SPECTACULAR GOLF
ONTARIO

THE MOST SCENIC AND CHALLENGING GOLF HOLES IN THE PROVINCE

Published by

PANACHE
P A N A C H E   P A R T N E R S

Panache Partners Canada Inc.
1424 Gables Court
Plano, TX 75075
469.246.6060
Fax: 469.246.6062
www.panache.com

Publishers: Brian G. Carabet and John A. Shand

Printed in Canada

Distributed by Independent Publishers Group
800.888.4741

PUBLISHER'S DATA

Spectacular Golf Ontario

Library of Congress Control Number: 2013933912

ISBN 13: 978-0-9832398-9-5
ISBN 10: 983239894

First Printing 2013

10 9 8 7 6 5 4 3 2 1

Right: Bigwin Island Golf Club, page 81

Previous Page: Turnberry Golf Club, page 217

Panache Partners, LLC, is dedicated to the restoration and conservation of the
environment. Our books are manufactured with strict adherence to an environmental
management system in accordance with ISO 14001 standards, including the use
of paper from mills certified to derive their products from well-managed forests.
We are committed to continued investigation of alternative paper products and
environmentally responsible manufacturing processes to ensure the preservation of our
fragile planet.

SPECTACULAR GOLF
ONTARIO

Mississaugua Golf and Country Club, page 137

FOREWORD

They say "home is where your heart is." For me, as a professional golfer who travels constantly and now makes my family's home in Utah, Ontario will always be home, both in a personal sense and as a golfer.

I have learned over the years that the more you travel, the more incredible places you visit, and the more golf courses you play around the world, the more you appreciate how those early influences have made you who you are. From first developing my love of the game on the driving range at Huron Oaks Golf Club in Sarnia to anticipating family vacations and golf with my dad and brothers at Taboo in Muskoka, Ontario's great golf courses have always had a huge influence on me, even when putting out to win the Masters.

Ontario is blessed with beautiful and spectacular countryside. This, coupled with some brilliant course designs, has helped make our province a golfer's paradise. With more than 800 golf courses to choose from, and 12 of the top 20 courses in Canada located in Ontario, there is quite literally a style, course, and challenge for everyone. I have seen firsthand how much players on Tour have enjoyed playing the Canadian Open at courses like Hamilton Golf & Country Club, along with occasions to play great courses like The National Golf Club of Canada and St. George's Golf and Country Club, and I am always proud to say that this is home for me.

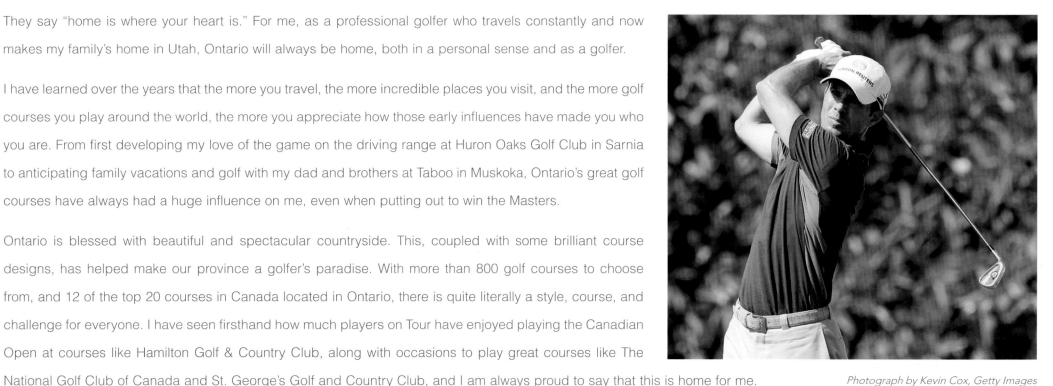

Photograph by Kevin Cox, Getty Images

Within the pages of *Spectacular Golf Ontario* are chronicled the magnificent courses and holes that have helped put the province on the golfing map. Whether located near a bustling big city or tucked away in Ontario's dazzling countryside, each of these courses possesses something special. For those who enjoy traveling to play some of the world's great golf courses, no list would be complete without a trip to Ontario. For those who call Ontario home, enjoy the fact that you have some of the best golf courses in the world right at your fingertips.

Yours truly,

Mike Weir

GOLF ASSOCIATION OF ONTARIO

Welcome to *Spectacular Golf Ontario*, a publication that we at the Golf Association of Ontario believe showcases the incredibly diverse selection of fantastic golf courses across the province; courses that are second to none. Opportunities to experience great golf are available to Ontarians and visitors in every part of the province. *Spectacular Golf Ontario* provides you with an enjoyable and memorable trip through some of Ontario's finest golf courses.

The Golf Association of Ontario is pleased to have the opportunity to be part of this beautiful publication. In addition to providing a lasting memory of our golf courses, our involvement will help in efforts to grow participation in the sport, assist the performance of our golfers, and support the Ontario golf industry.

Specific grassroots and development programs will all benefit from the exposure that the GAO receives in *Spectacular Golf Ontario*, including Golf in Schools, an interactive introduction to golf that reaches children in more than 800 schools across the province, and CN Future Links, a program that engages 6,000 children annually in the game. The GAO also helps prepare Ontario's best young golfers for the national and international competitive stages through the Team Ontario program, which develops the champions of tomorrow who will inspire new participants to take up the game.

I trust that as you browse through this wonderful book you will have an opportunity to see some of your favorite courses, your favorite golf holes, and perhaps find a few new ones that will make it onto your personal must-play list.

Golf is a game for the ages—a game for all ages—and Ontario offers wonderful golf courses for all who wish to play.

Enjoy *Spectacular Golf Ontario*.

Dave Mills
Executive Director
Golf Association of Ontario

GOLF
ASSOCIATION *of* ONTARIO

Photographs courtesy of Golf Association of Ontario

Eagles Nest Golf Club, page 109

CONTENTS

Wildfire Golf Club, page 71

Muskoka Bay Club, page 141

ONTARIO

Crosswinds Golf & Country Club, page 179

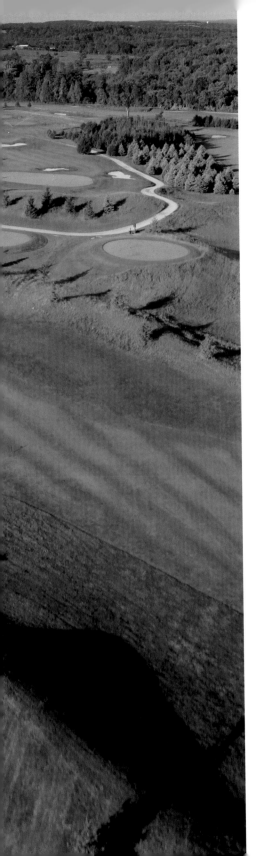

BAXTER CREEK
Golf Club

PAR 5 ◆ 484 YARDS

Fraserville, ON
705.932.8888
www.baxtercreekgolf.com

With nine water hazards in play on the course, the short but demanding par-5 17th at Baxter Creek Golf Club has three ponds. Two are strategically placed along the left side of this narrow fairway and the third completely surrounds the peninsula green. Golfers' confidence in their shot-making skills and keeping the ball right of center will provide an opportunity to reach the green in two. Risk/reward is ever present on this hole, as the second shot must be "all carry" of 200-plus yards to land softly on this medium-size green. Left, right, and far are all staked red and a penalty is the reward for one's bravado.

Hit the ball too far right from the tee box and you could be facing a difficult sidehill lie, with the second fairway water feature lurking threateningly to grab any errant sidehill shot.

Players who wish to play conservatively will find a lay up to a tight landing area left of the green as the best option for their second shot and an intelligent play. But beware, as there is a deep bunker 50 yards out in the middle of the fairway. Finding the sand in this hazard will create a great deal of anxiety for golfers of nearly any level, as the wedge shot must be perfect in distance to avoid the water and reach the green in regulation for a reasonable attempt at par. The green is true but breaks toward the water—which is everywhere.

Photograph by RC Media

BEACH GROVE
Golf & Country Club

18 HOLE

PAR 5 ◆ 546 YARDS

Tecumseh, ON
519.979.8090
www.beachgrove.net

Approaching the 18th green at Beach Grove Golf & Country Club, golfers have a wonderful view of the expansive Tudor-style clubhouse with sparkling Lake St. Clair in the background. It's a fitting conclusion to a round on this classic Stanley Thompson-designed golf course. Members and guests are reminded of the club's history, dating back to the early 1920s, and have a keen sense that with the finest amenities and state-of-the-art agronomy, the best of the modern era has been blended seamlessly with time-honored traditions. The family-oriented philosophy of the founding members lives on in the incomparable facilities, and on the golf course that is as playable and enjoyable with modern equipment as it was in the days of the hickory shaft.

Then, as now, Beach Grove's finishing hole requires course management, just as Thompson intended. The fairway rises away from the four tee boxes on this almost straightaway par 5 that moves slightly right to left near the green. Tall trees define the hole on both sides, and whether from the front tee at 445 yards or from the back tee at 546 yards, tee shots must favor the right side of the fairway. For most players it is a three-shot hole, and all approaches must contend with Thompson's imaginative bunkering. Two bunkers guard the right front and right side of the small green that is barely 5,000 square feet. On the other side is the virtual "sea of sand": multi-fingered with two grass islands and a peninsula that is six times larger than the green, starting at the front left and winding around to the back of the putting surface. A par here is memorable; a save from the "sea," unforgettable.

Photographs by Glenn Gervais

BEACON HALL
Golf Club

PAR 5 ◆ 580 YARDS

Aurora, ON
905.841.9122
www.beaconhall.com

Players from the elite to the amateur have stood in awe on Beacon Hall Golf Club's par-5 15th tee, known as one of golf's finest holes anywhere. A massive waste bunker offers a memory and lots of grill room conversation. The fairway moves to the right around the cavernous waste bunker and turns to the left. Players can bite off as much of the waste bunker as they can handle, allowing for a shorter layup shot. Sometimes it is worthwhile due to the narrowness of the second shot's landing area. But the real question is whether or not they can get it through the notch at the base of the huge dune on the left and cut off as much as 100 yards to the green. The successful reward is to set up an opportunity to go for the green in two and possibly a shot at eagle. It is the quintessential swing hole. A failed tee shot landing in the waste bunker will face several nasty scenarios, including grassy mounds or footprints from the day's previous golfers.

On the route around the right side the hole is a monster, with three demanding shots guaranteed. Through the cutoff, getting home is almost assured, though "almost" means a career right-to-left long iron or hybrid to the green. The hole location is unimportant at the tee, but grows in consequence as the player nears the green. The surface is busy and may well determine what club the player will hit for a second shot and whether or not to go for the green. The hole offers choices at every shot. The 15th is as good as it gets, or in the words of PGA Tour veteran Curt Byrum, "The 15th may be the best par 5 I have ever played."

Photograph courtesy of Beacon Hall Golf Club

BIGWIN ISLAND
Golf Club

PAR 5 ◆ 574 YARDS

Lake of Bays, ON
705.635.2582
www.bigwinisland.com

The Bigwin Inn first opened its doors in 1920, and right from the start guests enthusiastically embraced the lifestyle and spirit of the Roaring '20s. To this day, Bigwin Island—named for Ojibwa warrior and hunter Chief Joseph Big Wind—is known as the ultimate retreat, a sanctuary of relaxation and recreation in a spectacularly beautiful natural setting. And since the opening of Bigwin Island Golf Club, it is also renowned as one of golf's finest destinations.

Named the best new course in Canada in 2002, Carrick's masterpiece is reminiscent of the legendary Stanley Thompson's timeless style of accentuating the natural beauty of the landscape and creating unforgettable tee shots punctuated by large, flashy bunkers. Players are treated to a journey of over 7,000 yards through wooded corridors with granite outcrops and spectacular views at every turn. One of the most stunning is the look from the 18th tee.

Each hole at Bigwin Island Golf Club has an evocative name. The 18th's is The Lake of Bays. From the tee on this 574-yard par 5, the view of the lake—with the distant green seemingly tucked right up to the water's edge—and the islands in the distance is totally captivating. The longest hole on the course requires a solid tee shot to the fairway 100 feet below, between the lake and two large bunkers. The second shot must carry a large bunker fronting the second landing area, leaving a short third shot to a narrow green framed by luxuriant trees, the lake, and seven bunkers. Befitting the historic setting, the 18th is a classic.

Photograph © Clive Barber

BRAEBEN
Golf Course

PAR 5 ◆ 469 YARDS

Mississauga, ON
905.615.4653
www.mississauga.ca/portal/
discover/braebengolfcourse

Sharing the dramatic landforms that are prominent features of the famous links courses of the British Isles, BraeBen Golf Course features many of the natural challenges synonymous with true links designs: ever-present and changing winds, large greens, strategically placed pot bunkers, and fescue so deep that even the likes of Bubba Watson would find it difficult to hit from it.

Though it measures only 469 yards, don't let the distance of this par 5 fool you, as your drive must maneuver between the bunkers on both sides of the landing area as well as penal fescue down both sides of the hole. The 6th is all about accuracy, and a well-positioned first shot will set up an opportunity for reaching the green in regulation. Any errant ball missing the center of this narrow fairway, and course strategy must now come into play. Do not "guide" the second shot to avoid these hazards—swing free and easy and a legitimate opportunity for birdie will be your reward.

Course architect Ted Baker has a legacy of success in orchestrating natural terrain into the creation of enjoyable and playable designs throughout Ontario. Hit from the correct tee box, the one that suits your golf ability, and the result will be a memorable golf experience on one of Canada's premier links-style municipal golf courses.

Photograph by Peter A. Sellar

BRAMPTON
Golf Club

PAR 5 ◆ 468 YARDS

Brampton, ON
905.457.4443
www.bramptongolf.com

Brampton Golf Club, nearing its centennial, has aged gracefully, as has the "new" course designed by acclaimed Canadian architect C.E. "Robbie" Robinson that opened in 1963. The club is home to some of the province's best players—including 2012 Ontario Women's Amateur Champion Brittany Marchand—and has hosted some of Ontario's and Canada's premier tournaments. The challenging 6,558-yard layout has been the site of the Ontario Amateur, five CPGA Seniors championships, the CPGA Championship, and the Canadian Tour Players Championship. The club's fine amateur golfers, the players in the extensive junior programs, and all the members and guests benefit from the superb practice facilities that are among the best in the Greater Toronto Area.

Practice certainly pays off at the beautiful 17th hole. The green is not visible from the tee boxes, as the par 5 doglegs to the right along the floor of the Etobicoke Creek Valley. The hole is not overly long at 468 yards from the golds or 386 yards from the yellows, but it plays over the creek so club selection is key. The creek crosses the fairway at 240 yards from the back tees, with rough at the end of the fairway before the creek, so it calls for a shot of about 210 yards. Longer players can go for the elevated green on their second shot; those laying up must avoid the fairway bunker on the right and trees on the left.

Emulating his mentor Stanley Thompson, Robinson created large greens. The 17th is 35 yards deep, again putting the onus on club selection. Deep bunkers left and right guard the front of the green, with two more at the back of the green that slopes toward the front. The 17th is one of 18 very good reasons that Brampton Golf Club has stood the test of time.

Photograph courtesy of Brampton Golf Club

CARDINAL
Golf Club

10 HOLE

PAR 5 ◆ 561 YARDS

Newmarket, ON
905.841.7378
www.cardinalgolfclub.com

Cardinal Golf Club, the largest golf facility in Canada, features three championship courses as well as a challenging 18-hole executive course. In 2009, course architect Kevin Holmes created the premier course on the property, RedCrest. At 6,800 yards, this par-71 has incorporated the rolling terrain of the Holland Marsh Canal region and its meandering tributaries, bringing natural wetlands into play on 14 of the 18 holes. If maneuvering around these natural hazards wasn't difficult enough, the architect strategically placed hundreds of white sand bunkers in "ball capturing" locations from tee to green.

The 10th hole typifies the beauty and the beast of the course. As players stand on the tee box, they are faced with an accepting fairway but must be aware of the prevailing westerly winds. Should the wind be gusting, golfers may require a bit of luck, as there are well-positioned fairway and greenside bunkers awaiting any mishit ball. Playing to the right side of the fairway allows for the easiest second shot on this difficult par 5 and provides the only chance for the long hitters to get home in two. The second shot is the most challenging, as there is an expansive marshland on this sharp dogleg right to carry before finding the safe landing area. Any ball hit too far left from the tee will require a long, 200-yard-plus carry over the water feature. Once over the marshland, a comfortable short-iron approach to the two-tiered green remains. An approach shot to the elevated green cannot be long, as a player will be forced to negotiate a delicate flop shot to this downward sloping green. If you do not attempt the impossible on this hole and play smart, the reward is par or better.

Photograph by Brent Long

CARLETON
Golf & Yacht Club

Manotick, ON
613.692.3531
www.carletongolf.com

The setting is so idyllic that it is not surprising Carleton Golf & Yacht Club was created as the centerpiece of a residential community. Just a 30-minute drive south of Ottawa, on the shore of the historic Rideau River, the location is not only ideal but so too is the terrain and the unspoiled natural surroundings. A residential community on a championship golf course is now commonplace worldwide. However, when the first nine holes of Carleton Golf & Yacht Club opened in 1963, it was just the second golf course purposely built as an integral part of a real estate development in North America. The second nine opened in 1966 and the members bought it the following year, operating it as a member-owned, private, not-for-profit club ever since. In its first half-century, the course has matured and evolved but never strayed from its raison d'être: a focal point for families and friends.

The 5th hole is a short par 5 full of opportunity. The tees—489 yards from the back tees, 411 yards from the forward—are set in a narrow, tree-lined alley. A strong drive down the left side can catch the down slope and gain extra distance and a good chance to reach the green in two. Most players play a lay up between the two fairway bunkers and favor the right side to open up the best angle into the green. The small, two-tiered putting surface is guarded by large bunkers, a slope on the left side, and is surrounded by thick rough. The ambitious will need to carry the front-left bunker to find the green; a tough shot, as the green is narrow and angled right to left. This seemingly simple hole invites aggressive play, but those who overplay their hands will quickly add to their score.

Photograph by Scott MacLeod, www.FlagstickGolfPhotography.com

CHERRY HILL
Club

18 HOLE

PAR 5 ◆ 554 YARDS

Ridgeway, ON
905.894.1122
www.cherryhillclub.ca

The 18th at Cherry Hill Club is a solid finishing hole that brings players uphill toward the clubhouse. Off the tee, the fairway is constricted by a trio of bunkers, two on the left and one on the right, at the point where it makes a pronounced bend to the left. The distance to this narrow chute is tricky, presenting the temptation to play over it even though the shot is beyond the scope of most players. This combination of distance, narrow fairway, bunkers, and trees tips the risk/reward scale for a bold tee-shot clearly to the side of risk.

Once past the chute, you are confronted by a long fairway, playing toward a relatively large, undulating green that is well protected by bunkers on the right side of the fairway itself and that nearly encircle the front side of the green. Careful club selection allows players to set up their third shot from an advantageous position, important since noticeable mounding on the green makes for interesting pin placements and puts a premium on the approach shot.

Play well on this hole and adjourn to the clubhouse to savor a game well finished. If your game succumbs to the challenges hole 18 presents, you can find solace in the knowledge that more than one pro has suffered the same fate with bogeys, double-bogeys, and even worse appearing on scorecards, even in championship play. Either way, the 18th provides a striking conclusion to an always memorable round.

Photographs by John Gall

CREDIT VALLEY
Golf and Country Club

PAR 5 ◆ 505 YARDS

Mississauga, ON
905.275.2505
www.creditvalleygolf.com

The 8th at Credit Valley Golf and Country Club is a long par 5 with a relatively narrow fairway that curves gradually in a slight dogleg left all the way from tee to green. Well-treed on both sides, the hole dictates that errant shots are trouble. The trees also encroach on the fairway at the two-thirds point. Hitting out of a chute, your tee ball should target the right side of the fairway, as everything left of center kicks off to the left, blocking a second shot to the green. A perfect drive will leave a 250-yard approach to the slightly elevated green.

Four bunkers surround this green, all strategically placed and resulting in a narrowed fairway and constricted approach just short of the green. Place a ball too far off the putting surface and an up-and-down will be almost impossible. Many golfers will be forced to lay up—stay to the right side of the fairway to avoid being blocked out by a large maple that stands guard 75 yards short and left of the green. The green is centered by a mound, which makes the correct distance imperative. It also slopes left to right, and a ball landing on the correct side of the pin placement to avoid the mound will have a good opportunity for a one or two-putt for a well deserved birdie or par.

Photograph courtesy of Credit Valley Golf and Country Club

DRAGON'S FIRE

Golf Club

18 HOLE

PAR 5 ◆ 533 YARDS

Flamborough, ON
905.690.0069
www.dragonsfiregolf.com

Playability, shot values, and visual aesthetics are the cornerstones of great course design, and the public Dragon Fire's Golf Club qualifies on all counts. It measures over 7,202 yards from the back tees, but with six tees on each hole, it is playable for every level and age of golfer. The variations are as distinct as the holes are individual, with the blue tees at 6,639 yards, the popular whites at 6,161 yards, and the reds at 5,085 yards. Built on top of a hill, the front nine goes around the outside of the course and the back nine on the inside, creating a natural flow. The big, wide fairways and large greens are bentgrass and meet all USGA specifications; their proportions ideally suit the towering trees and vast surrounding landscape. Dragon's Fire was built by a golfer, for golfers.

The home hole is a magnificent risk/reward, reachable par 5. The 533-yard dogleg right traces the edge of the large pond almost the entire length of the fairway. From all tees, players don't have to carry over any water, but they definitely have to flirt with it. A tee shot that flies the bunker on the right sets up a short second into the green. The safer route is left, but the more that side is favored the closer it is to the two fairway bunkers and the further it is from the putting surface. Layup shots have to contend with two bunkers short left, and the pond right. The undulating green slopes back to front, so any approaches past the pin leave quick downhill putts. Players soon discover that, even though it's the final hole, there is plenty of fire left in the Dragon.

Photograph courtesy of Dragon's Fire Golf Club

ELMIRA
Golf Club

PAR 5 ◆ 543 YARDS

Elmira, ON
519.669.1652
www.elmiragolfclub.com

Steeped in the culture of the surrounding Mennonite settlements, Elmira Golf Club embodies the area's uniqueness and its warm sense of community. Set in the rich, rolling farmland of Southern Ontario, 60 miles west of Toronto and just north of Kitchener-Waterloo, the club has been a focal point for social gatherings and fine golf for more than half a century. Through the vision, determination, and two years of sheer physical effort by the original members and volunteers—the weekend stone collecting parties are now part of local lore—the golf course's first nine holes opened in 1965. The second nine opened in 1973, completing the picturesque layout of undulating, tree-lined fairways with Larches Creek running through.

Water and trees play vital roles on the strategic 5th hole, a well-designed par 5 that plays 543 yards from the back tees, 452 and 446 yards from the forward tee decks.

The pond in front of the back two tees helps players focus on the hill rising to the landing area and the tall trees defining the fairway on both sides. The 5th usually plays into the wind, a consideration for longer hitters attempting to reach the green in two. The fairway narrows as it approaches the putting surface that is protected by small but well-placed front bunkers left and right. There are mounds to the right and back of the green, which is 44 yards deep but relatively narrow. The first of just two par 5s at Elmira is a chance to kickstart the round, but par is not a gimme.

Photographs courtesy of Elmira Golf Club

GRANITE
Golf Club

PAR 5 ◆ 543 YARDS

Stouffville, ON
905.642.4416
www.granitegolfclub.ca

As the host club to major events such as the Canadian Women's Amateur and the National Junior Championships, it's easy to see why Granite Golf Club is a great test of the game. This is evident on the challenging, long, uphill par-5 9th hole, a superb test of golf in every sense, as the dogleg left hole requires positioning on every shot to have any chance at par. From the tee, marshland stretches from the tee box to 150 yards across the front of the tee area. The correct line for the drive is to aim toward the right center of the fairway, which avoids the large left fairway bunker 250 yards out and provides a good line for a rescue club or long iron to a narrow landing area on the right side of the fairway. Fescue and trees along both sides of this narrow approach can be trouble, and you must avoid getting too close to the large maple located 100 yards out from the green on the right. A shot too far left will create a difficult angle to this small, elevated putting surface, which is guarded by deep bunkers front and back right. Keep it on the fairway.

As on most of the greens on Granite Golf Club, be wary of the undulations, which can be deceiving if you do not take the time to read from the front and back of the putting line. A ball above the pin or a sidehill putt and a three-putt is not rare. The green is fair and fast, so judge your line and weight and a one-putt will be your prize.

Photograph © Clive Barber

GRANITE
Golf Club

PAR 5 ◆ 500 YARDS

Stouffville, ON
905.642.4416
www.granitegolfclub.ca

Granite Golf Club is more than a world-class course; it's a warm and relaxed atmosphere that welcomes entire families and every level of golfer to enjoy a round of golf and the club's many amenities.

Truly a classic in hole design, Granite Golf Club's magnificent par-5 13th demands accuracy and ball placement for every shot. Water on the left, trees on the right, and six bunkers lie in wait to entrap the approach shot. On this sharp dogleg left hole, a drive down the middle from the back tees of 250 yards will avoid the water hazards that are veiled behind a thin line of trees along the left. Shots hit too far right will find the forest of trees and will greatly diminish the opportunity for par.

For many, a second shot entails getting out of trouble and facing the realization that there is still a long way to go—reaching the green in regulation is now out of the question. Play conservatively, know your shot-making ability, and play "within yourself." Once in position with a short approach to this elevated, narrow green, walk up and take a look at the pin placement and examine the subtle contours of the green before you make your club selection; balls hit past the pin will face a fast and difficult downhill putt. Walk away with par and you can confidently play the finishing holes with the knowledge that you have played a championship hole with success.

Photographs © Clive Barber

HUNTERS POINTE
Golf Course

18 HOLE

PAR 5 ◆ 538 YARDS

Welland, ON
877.714.4659
www.hpgolf.ca

Hunters Pointe Golf Course has been consistently ranked among the best courses in the province and one of the great replicas of links-style golf since opening in 2000. The scenic course runs parallel to the historic Welland Canal, where large grain and ore ships navigate the series of locks that connect Lake Ontario with Lake Erie and are a constant companion on many of the holes.

Lightning-fast greens, white sand bunkers, and a long history of top-level conditioning help this course feel like a classic Scottish links course. A rolling landscape, testing dunes, and deep pot bunkers, combined with fescue, bentgrass, and the occasional tree, assist in targeting. With the addition of seven ponds, course architect Graham Cooke & Associates created a design that has become a favorite test for amateur, collegiate, and professional championships.

The finishing hole at Hunters Pointe is as breathtaking as it is daunting. At 538 yards from the back tees, this par 5 is reminiscent of the finishing hole at The Stadium Course at TPC Scottsdale. A player standing on the tee box is forced to pick the correct line and perfect a drive that carries the slender inlet that traverses the fairway. Also try to avoid the lateral water hazard parallel along the right side of the fairway. The second shot is risk/reward. The safe option is to target the 100-yard marker, as the water feature meanders back in front of the green. For those with confidence, a well-executed wood will carry the water but be "high and soft" with this approach, as the 18th green is one of the hardest surfaces to hold. Adding to the scenic beauty are mounded knolls, windblown fescue, deep greenside pot bunkers, and a unique array of diving birds, all helping to create an unforgettable golf hole.

Photograph courtesy of Hunters Pointe Golf Course

LOCH MARCH
Golf & Country Club

PAR 5 ◆ 510 YARDS

Kanata, ON
613.839.5885
www.lochmarch.com

Although Loch March Golf & Country Club is in the heart of the Canadian Shield and plays to 7,000 yards with plenty of elevation change, it is walkable. In this classic design, the greens are close to the next tee box, yet from the five sets of tees there are only rare glimpses of other holes. There is no housing, or other man-made intrusions, on the 300 acres. In fact, at some points there are up to eight acres of verdant forest between holes. The original design has been slightly refined as the course has grown in and matured, and is ranked among the top 12 public courses in Ontario. Loch March's refinements have added to the enjoyment of scratch and average players, juniors, seniors, and newcomers.

In its own splendid isolation, the 6th hole is a great par 5 from all five tees, playing as long as 510 yards and as short as 389 yards. A gentle dogleg left, it is tight on that side but has plenty of room down the right. A creek crosses the fairway at 300 yards from the back tee, with the slope into the water starting at 290 yards, so a tee shot well short of the hazard is a good play. That leaves a level lie and a 200 to 215-yard shot up a fairway that climbs 20 feet to the green. The landing area for second shots is deep but narrow, with a bunker on the right, woods left. It is reachable, but plays uphill and into the prevailing wind. The green is not bunkered but two-tiered, sloping front to back to accept long shots, and sits in a bowl. Large banks on both sides help errant shots roll onto the green; those hitting the wrong side of the slope are likely lost. Enticing risks, great rewards.

Photographs by Michelle Valberg

THE MAD RIVER
Golf Club

PAR 5 ◆ 512 YARDS

Creemore, ON
705.428.3673
www.madriver.ca

The 13th hole at The Mad River Golf Club is a relatively short, 512-yard par 5, but it presents the golfer with a variety of challenging strategic options. Played from the back tee, the shot requires a drive of nearly 200 yards over wetlands with dense woods hugging the right side of the hole. This forces the eye left toward the church pew bunkers and a much longer carry to reach the fairway. Getting home in two requires a shot of 230 to 250 yards to a plateau green that sits nearly 50 feet above the fairway. Too short, and the ball will find one of two deep bunkers that lie a dozen feet below the putting surface. Too long, and the player will face an unnerving bunker shot or pitch to a narrow green that slopes away from the shot.

Almost as heroic is a second shot to the landing area right of the green—lower and shorter than the direct route—that gives players a full view down the length of the green for their third. More conservative still is a well-placed mid-iron second shot. Accuracy is essential here to avoid uneven lies along the left side of the fairway and a fall-off on the right into thick rough. The approach demands a well-executed wedge that must take into account the tight lie, exact distance, elevated green, and swirling winds. Like most holes at Mad River, par or better on the 13th requires that every shot be played with a combination of skill and confidence.

Photographs by Hilton Tudhope

THE MAD RIVER
Golf Club

PAR 5 ◆ 606 YARDS

Creemore, ON
705.428.3673
www.madriver.ca

The Mad River Golf Club's 17th is one of the most dramatic golf holes in Ontario. From the back tee, with its expansive views over rolling farmland and out to the waters of Georgian Bay, the hole unfolds 606 yards and falls 74 feet to its lowest point. From any tee box, trust and strategy are required before a shot is made. Dense wetlands line the entire left side while deep woods lie along the opposite edge, punctuated by mounds and bunkers right of the landing area. The mid-to-long-iron second shot plays slightly downhill toward the corner of the dogleg, which brings the large pond on the right into range. Three bunkers guard the left side of the fairway some 60 to 100 yards short of the green, waiting to capture the long hitter looking for a shorter approach to the green.

From the ideal landing area, golfers are left with a short iron or wedge to a slightly elevated green. It is a surprisingly challenging shot to one of the smallest greens on the course. The bunker front right is well below the putting surface, and any ball further off line will find the pond. Shots favoring the left side, if not precise, will settle on a steep upslope punctuated by hummocks and depressions and covered in deep rough. Even the most accurately placed shot must deal with a green that slopes from front to back, then falls off sharply to the back and right. Few members complain about par on the 17th.

Photograph by Hilton Tudhope

MAGNA
Golf Club

HOLE 14

PAR 5 ◆ 536 YARDS

Aurora, ON
905.726.3456
www.magnagolf.com

Magna Golf Club's Doug Carrick-designed, award-winning, 7,300-yard layout has been the home and host to many of Canada's—and the world's—most influential business personalities as well as the likes of Tiger Woods, Ernie Els, and Annika Sörenstam. This exclusive facility is a synthesis of nature and design, as Carrick has incorporated the rolling hills of the region into a course with wide fairways, striking contoured greens, and immense bunkering.

The 14th hole is the epitome of risk versus reward. Situated high atop the Oak Ridges Moraine, this majestic par 5 tees off dramatically from the highest point on the Magna property. Measuring 536 yards from the tips, the hole forces players to make a series of great shots if they are to walk away with birdie. A draw aimed at the middle of the fairway is the ideal shot for most players, while long hitters can take aim over a group of three diabolically placed bunkers surrounded by fescue along the left edge of the

fairway. Trouble is found along the entire left side of the hole, which tumbles off into a fescue-covered oblivion.

If the tee shot finds the flat shelf at the bottom of the 65-plus-foot drop in elevation, the player is then left with the decision to go for the green from over 200 yards, or lay up. A miss left of the green will hopefully find a soft landing in the bunker. Short right will leave a tricky bunker shot, while a pin-high miss right leaves the player with an awkward downhill pitch shot from thick rough. Players missing the green long will find themselves hunting for their ball in deep fescue. The approach must be well placed, as the green itself slopes from back to front, with subtle ripples and rolls making even the shortest putts seem impossible.

Photograph courtesy of Magna Golf Club

MIDLAND
Golf & Country Club

PAR 5 ◆ 527 YARDS

Midland, ON
705.526.5822
www.midlandgolfcc.com

More than 90 years ago, businessman and visionary James Playfair established Midland Golf & Country Club in the heart of Ontario's beautiful Georgian Bay area. Designed by Wellington Nicol Thompson, older brother of the legendary course architect Stanley Thompson, the semi-private Midland course opened in 1919 and to this day is among the province's finest. In the early 1990s, Doug Carrick—one of the game's leading modern architects who worked with Stanley—initiated a long-range plan of capital improvements that have maintained and enhanced Midland's treasured heritage and its classic Thompson design. The collective talent of both architects is on full display at the 15th hole, aptly named Big Chief.

An essential element of enduring course design is that there is no trickery. From the elevated tee boxes, the challenges of the par-5 15th are clear. Whether playing from the blues at 527 yards, the whites at 501 yards, or the yellows at 436 yards,

all players equally enjoy the stunning view and the options Thompson masterfully provided. Players must decide between the risks—and reward—of hitting driver and hitting a shorter club to ensure finding the fairway. Those entertaining the challenge of reaching the green in two must avoid a pair of ideally placed fairway bunkers, at 250 yards on the left and 280 yards on the right.

Golfers playing Big Chief as a three-shot hole must be wary of the bunker 70 yards from the putting surface. All shots into the green must skirt the surrounding bushes and the bunker guarding the left side. Overly aggressive approaches can run off the back, leaving a difficult up and down. Midland's 15th is a classic old-style par 5 brought skillfully into the modern era.

Photographs by Jody Juras

MILL RUN
Golf Club

PAR 5 ◆ 567 YARDS

Uxbridge, ON
800.465.8633
www.golfmillrun.com

Mill Run Golf Club is a unique, full-service golf facility with a difference. Here, all the amenities of a private club are available to the public. The club prides itself on having an option for every type of golfer, be it an equity membership for those looking to call Mill Run home or public green fee rates that provide tremendous value for pay-as-you-play golfers. Nestled in the rolling hills surrounding Uxbridge in the beautiful region of Durham, Mill Run provides both challenging golf and great scenery. Befitting its idyllic location, the course is completing its Audubon Certification. It also received the 2012 Uxbridge Environmental Heroes Award in recognition of an extensive creek diversion project that protected nearly 680 yards of stream bank and restored more than nine acres of aquatic habitat.

Annually ranked as one of the most difficult in the Durham region and Greater Toronto Area, the par-5 opening hole on The Wheel nine provides a formidable start to any round. The tree-lined, 567-yard double-dogleg crosses the Pefferlaw Brook three times, requiring three well-placed shots for a chance at par or better. Golfers whose shots stray into the woods must heed the warning signs and avoid the quicksand.

Tee shots from all four tee boxes—the hole plays to 417 yards from the forward tee—should favor the left side of the fairway. Only the longest hitters can entertain getting home in two. Most players opt for a layup second shot to just in front of the brook, leaving an approach shot between 120 to 150 yards. The braver can play their second shot over the brook to the small island landing area. That leaves a short wedge, but still not an easy shot as the green is elevated, tricky, and two-tiered.

Photograph by Stuart Brindle

MISSISSAUGUA
Golf and Country Club

12 HOLE

PAR 5 ◆ 586 YARDS

Mississauga, ON
905.278.4857
www.mississauguagolf.com

The fifth of six Canadian Opens hosted by Mississaugua Golf and Country Club is remembered as the one that got away from Jack Nicklaus. In the final round of the '65 Open, on the par-5 12th fondly known as Big Chief by members, Nicklaus went for the green in two, but came up just short as his ball landed in the creek that cuts in front of the green. With one foot on a rock, he played the ball out of the water, chipped from the gallery, and two-putted for bogey. Gene Littler laid up, chipped on, and one-putted for birdie. Littler went on to win by a single stroke.

For more than a century, Mississaugua Golf and Country Club members and guests have grappled with the intriguing risk/reward options of going for it or laying up for a conservative approach to birdie. There's always something a little different to consider, and that's what makes it one of the exceptional holes in Canadian golf. Some days you might come up short off the tee, others you could find yourself in the rough, or sometimes there's a downhill lie on the fairway and you wouldn't want to take such a risk. Other days, it's downwind and you can be more aggressive.

The hole has been lengthened 51 yards since Nicklaus played it, and at 586 yards it is the longest hole on a course that now plays 7,109 yards, par-71 from the tips. With a solitary bunker lying at the back of the green and a rumpled fairway lined by magnificent trees, Big Chief is a shining example of parkland golf within the breathtaking Credit River Valley that is Mississaugua's heart and soul.

Photograph @ Clive Barber

POINTE WEST
Golf Club

18 HOLE

PAR 5 ◆ 500 YARDS

Amherstburg, ON
519.736.8623
www.pointewestgolf.com

In an ideal setting for a classic links-style golf course, celebrated architect Thomas McBroom created a walkable layout where each hole is memorable, offering its own unique challenges and pleasures. Fashioning gently rolling slopes and slight elevation changes, McBroom designed firm fairways that weave through old-growth timber, complemented by undulating bentgrass greens. The southernmost private golf club in Canada, just a short drive to Windsor and Detroit and a few miles north of Lake Erie, Pointe West Golf Club is also one of the country's finest. Established in 1989, the course plays from 5,076 yards back to 6,631 yards from five sets of tees, with five par 5s and five par 3s, providing an enjoyable test for golfers of all ages and skill levels.

The 18th hole challenges every aspect of a player's game: power, accuracy, and finesse. This 500-yard par 5 is a very difficult driving hole, with out-of-bounds on the heavily treed right, trees and a creek on the left. For the longer golfers hoping to reach the green in two, the landing area is tight with another creek on the right. For most players the second shot is a lay up, but a challenging shot nevertheless with a long iron or hybrid club. The third shot is not easy. The deep, kidney-shaped green slopes back to front, with a camel's back in the middle, and is guarded by a pond on the left that starts 150 yards from the front. Players going to a left pin risk spinning the ball back into the water. A large bunker dominates the right side of the manicured putting surface, and the bunker behind the green poses a very challenging shot down the bentgrass slope. The 18th hole is a fitting conclusion to a superbly designed course.

Photographs by Chiaroscuro Arts

RENFREW
Golf Club

PAR 5 ◆ 476 YARDS

Renfrew, ON
613.432.2485
www.renfrewgolf.com

The Old Stone House logo of Renfrew Golf Club reminds members and daily players of the history and tradition of a club that dates back to 1929. Home to the original family that farmed the lovely acreage in the Bonnechere River watershed, the house stood between the 10th tee and 18th fairway and served as a clubhouse for decades. Its honored place as the logo reflects the club's rich heritage and respect for the past even while embracing the future. Like the first family, the club members play an active role in the community 50 minutes northwest of Ottawa. Fundraising tournaments are annual events because the traditional park land course is walkable and welcoming, yet challenging. All 18 green complexes were completely redesigned in 2000 with large bentgrass putting surfaces, free-form bunkers, mounding, and rolling surrounds. With mature trees defining fairways and strategically placed bunkers and hazards, a par-71 round on Renfrew's 6,501-yard layout is a superb score.

The subtleties of the design are evident on the deceptively difficult 18th. From all four elevated tees, the par 5 appears straightforward. Measuring 476 yards from the championship tees, 431 yards from the forward tees, it might even be considered short. But the landing area is narrow, and not only slopes from right to left but also downhill. The longest hitters might catch the down slope and have only a mid-iron into the green, but most players will have an awkward stance for their second shots, making a lay up a wise choice. The large green is at the top of a slope that begins 150 yards down the fairway and two bunkers guard the front, curving around to almost the mid-point of the putting surface. Like Renfrew's two other par 5s, the 18th has its risks and rewards.

Photograph by Scott MacLeod, www.FlagstickGolfPhotography.com

SILVER LAKES
Golf & Conference Centre

PAR 5 ◆ 531 YARDS

East Gwillimbury, ON
800.465.7888
www.silverlakesgolf.com

Continually rated as one of the top public courses in the Greater Toronto Area by the media and those who play, Silver Lakes Golf & Conference Centre's four-star championship golf course is reminiscent of the lush courses of the Carolinas. The course's layout encompasses an abundance of deciduous and coniferous trees, and the adjoining wetlands of the Holland River create beauty as well as myriad hazards for wayward shots.

One of the longest courses in Ontario, measuring 7,029 yards from the back of the five tee boxes, its signature hole takes in all the elements of Silver Lakes' majesty with water, large trees, and strategically placed bunkering. At 531 yards, you will have to be a power hitter to carry your tee shot the 265 yards over a lake that fronts the tee box. Even from the blue tees, most players still necessitate a minimum 200-yard shot to be safe. Aim your drive to the left side of the fairway, but too far left and you'll find yourself behind a large maple that protects any attempt to reach the green in two.

There is a good opportunity for birdie, but lose your shot and a bogey is your return, as this green is well protected by a strategically placed bunker on the left and a deep bunker and water on the right, creating a constricted approach angle. Always look up at the surrounding trees for the direction the wind is blowing, as it's easy to be fooled by the stillness of the air. A proper lofted club to keep the ball under the influence of the wind and having the ball rest below the pin will avoid a treacherous downhill putt on this long and narrow putting surface.

Photographs courtesy of Silver Lake Golf & Conferene Centre

ST. ANDREW'S
East Golf & Country Club

PAR 5 ◆ 525 YARDS

Stouffville, ON
905.640.4444
www.standrewseast.com

Named after Toronto's original St. Andrew's Golf Club—the host of two Canadian Opens and the first public golf facility to be so honored—St. Andrew's East Golf & Country Club opened in 1988 on one of Canadian golf's most picturesque and natural settings. Conveniently situated 30 minutes north of the nation's largest city, St. Andrew's East offers a dramatic view of the Greater Toronto skyline. This meticulously maintained championship course seems a world apart. Renowned course architect Rene Muylaert, designer of more than 38 courses throughout Ontario, etched this 6,805-yard masterpiece that has since been refined by award-winning architect Doug Carrick and his Carrick Design team.

Like classic links in the British Isles, the holes at St. Andrew's East are given evocative names. The 9th is no exception, appropriately named Signature. This par 5 brings players back to the clubhouse that's set upon the Oak Ridges moraine, the highest point of land between Lake Ontario to the south and Lake Simcoe to the north. The tee shot holds every player's attention. Nine sand bunkers frame the uphill challenge that plays longer than the scorecard's 525 yards. Trouble lurks approximately 290 yards off the tee, a hazard in the form of a lake that comes into play on three of St. Andrew's golf holes.

After a prudent lay up over the water, approaches must be precise to the expansive horseshoe-shaped green shared with the 15th hole. This double green is yet another respectful nod to Scotland's original Royal & Ancient Golf Club, which pioneered the use of double greens. Before facing their challenging putts, players would best forget that the 9th green lies in full view of members and their guests relaxing along the clubhouse deck.

Photograph by David Goldsman

ST. ANDREW'S
East Golf & Country Club

10 HOLE

PAR 5 ♦ 556 YARDS

Stouffville, ON
905.640.4444
www.standrewseast.com

Since Highland Pipers marched down the first fairway during the grand opening in 1988, St. Andrew's East Golf & Country Club has offered a superb golfing experience. Boasting outstanding conditions and facilities with unparalleled panoramic views, the 375 member-owners take pride in four-hour rounds on a championship layout, along with the fact that there are no tee times or outside events allowed. St. Andrew's East pays homage to golf's origins throughout the course, including the singular experience of six par 3s, six par 4s, and six par 5s, with two of the par 5s back-to-back at the turn.

The 10th is aptly named Outward Bound. This solid par 5 plays to a robust 556 yards from the back tees and 512 yards from the front, gently doglegging left to right against a lushly forested backdrop. Outward Bound presents an opportunity to make a birdie with a well-placed tee shot skirting the lake guarding the fairway's right side, past a large bunker with islands of fescue. A narrow entrance to the well-bunkered and deceptively elevated green usually discourages players from going for the green in two. When played as a true three-shot par 5, the second shot requires a lay up just short of a severe dip in front of the green not visible from the fairway.

With 18 distinctly different holes, the course is never repetitive. For more than a quarter of a century, St. Andrew's East has created its own traditions by providing members and their guests with variety, challenge, and, most importantly, enjoyment.

Photograph by David Goldsman

SUTTON CREEK
Golf Club

PAR 5 ◆ 489 YARDS

Essex, ON
519.726.6900
www.suttoncreekgolf.com

When Sutton Creek Golf Club opened in 1990, it signaled a new direction for public golf in Windsor-Essex County in southwestern Ontario. A park land design, Sutton Creek plays hard and fast, with lightning-quick greens at the end of perfectly manicured fairways. The 18-hole layout has 60 strategically placed bunkers, seven expansive ponds, and the county's McLaren Drain winding through it. With a well-designed mix of short, medium-length, and long holes, strategy is at a premium. At 6,792 yards from the back tees, the par-72 course presents a true test of golf as it was meant to be played. However, the four sets of tees and generous landing areas make it an enjoyable experience for everyone. Sutton Creek is truly bold, beautiful, and breathtaking all at once; a brand of golf rarely experienced.

At 489 yards, the 18th hole is a relatively short par 5, but numbers on scorecards can be deceiving. The tee shot is open with mounding down the left side and small trees down the right—this is where the real test begins. If long hitters hope to go for it, their tee shots must trace the right side, leaving a hybrid or long iron in. Second shots must carry a large lake to an island green that slopes from back to front. Any layup shots must avoid the fairway bunkers on the left side and the lake on the right. Third-shot approaches to the island green must negotiate bunkers left, front, and right, and the intimidating "armor" stones along the water's edge. The 18th hole at Sutton Creek Golf Club is visually stunning, challenging, and in every respect a fitting finale to a beautiful golf course.

Photographs courtesy of Sutton Creek Golf Club

VESPRA HILLS
Golf Club

PAR 5 ◆ 562 YARDS

Springwater Township, ON
705.721.5831
www.vesprahillsgolfclub.com

The youngest of the three nines at Vespra Hills Golf Club, Still Valley is often affectionately described as "Carnoustie meets Mexico" for its links-like fescue and rolling fairways, and its Los Cabos-inspired sand features. The construction was overseen by Cinder Warren, daughter of the designer of the Sand Hills and Homestead nines, G. Mac Frost, and aided by superintendent Dave Caldwell and a talented team of shapers. Opening in 2006 to rave reviews, the 3,461-yard, par-36 layout is the most challenging of the three nines. However, like all 27 Vespra Hills holes, there are four sets of tee decks, allowing players to select their level of challenge. Winding through the valley at the north end of the property, Still Valley incorporates sound environmental practices and innovative use of the natural soils, water flow, and sandy patches that are sculpted into numerous features on the course.

The finishing hole on the Still Valley nine is an adventure, rewarding shot-making skills, length, and well-thought-out strategy. This long—562 yards from the tips, 463 yards from the forward tee—par 5 requires a tee shot that follows the tree line on the right to somewhere just short of the "target" bunkers. From there the fairway narrows, so the prudent play is a shot to around the 150-yard marker. Approach shots are straight up the hill, known for its distinctive "steps." The grass on the upslopes is longer than on the flat steps, so misjudged shots can prove costly. A big bunker on the right and thick forest on the left guard the elevated green, and a large mound defines the back of the putting surface. The 9th is a strong climax to the Still Valley nine.

Photograph courtesy of Vespra Hills Golf Club

WILDFIRE
Golf Club

PAR 5 ◆ 550 YARDS

Lakefield, ON
705.877.9453
www.golfwildfire.com

Wildfire Golf Club, established in 1999, is a private golf course that encapsulates the richness of the surrounding land's sparkling lakes, deciduous and conifer forests, wetlands and creeks, and rolling terrain. One of Canada's most accomplished and internationally respected course architects—and recipient of six *Golf Digest* awards for best new Canadian course—Thomas McBroom was the natural choice to create this masterpiece, and in the summer of 2003 Wildfire opened to rave reviews.

A great finishing hole, this par 5 rounds the corner of a long dogleg left to provide a stunning view of the elegant, cottage-style clubhouse, named best new clubhouse in Canada in 2006 by *Fairways* magazine. A player's tee shot should favor the right middle of the fairway, while a lay up left of the furthest greenside bunker is the ideal second shot target. For long hitters who have confidence in their swing and wish to have a chance for birdie, a well-placed shot that hugs the left side of the fairway is the only option. Too aggressive, and this line will bring into play the tall fescue, well-placed trees, and large granite boulder that protect the left corner.

The approach shot to the green is as intimidating as it gets. Miss left, and a very delicate bunker shot or pitch straight toward the water is required. A mishit will end up in the pond, where bogey or worse will be your final score of the day. At 550 yards from the championship tees, the classic McBroom risk/reward hole is a perfect ending to a beautiful course.

Photographs © Clive Barber

AMBASSADOR
Golf Club

PAR 4 ◆ 489 YARDS

Windsor, ON
519.966.2425
www.ambassadorgolfclub.com

The quality of a golf course can be assessed in many ways. Most important are the level of championships contested and the popularity among the finest players and recreational enthusiasts alike. By any measure, Ambassador Golf Club is among the game's finest. Just six years after opening for play, Ambassador hosted the 2011 Canadian Tour Championship. The layout, designed by award-winning architect Thomas McBroom, has also hosted the 2010 Ontario Senior Men's Amateur, the 2009 Canadian Men's College Championships, and the 2008 Ontario Women's Mid-Amateur Championship. On 200 acres of relatively uneventful Southern Ontario landscape, McBroom sculpted an undulating masterpiece, a public course set behind the privacy of a man-made berm.

The 6th plays as the most difficult hole on this challenging but fair 7,033-yard McBroom design. From the four tee boxes—black, gold, pewter, and ivory—all players are fully engaged by the hole's length and imposing left-side bunker. Playing from the 329-yard ivory tee back to 489 yards from the black, the 6th is slightly uphill with a generous landing area guarded by the bunker and fescue on both sides. Ideal tee shots that carry that left bunker—235 yards from the black tee, 170 yards from the pewter tee—take advantage of the fairway's left-to-right slope that propels the shot forward.

The first of three bunkers on the right can be reached from the ivory, pewter, and gold tees. From any tee, players are faced with a long, slightly uphill second shot, but with the prevailing wind at their backs. The green is large—44 yards deep and 26 yards wide—and protected by deep bunkers on the right that feature the very playable Ohio White sand. Sloping back to front with undulations and three tiers, the green presents the final test, where a par usually picks up a stroke on the field.

Photograph © Clive Barber

BARRIE
Country Club

18 HOLE

PAR 4 ◆ 486 YARDS

Barrie, ON
705.728.4802
www.barriecountryclub.com

Originally a six-hole layout, the century-old Barrie Country Club was expanded to a nine-hole course by the internationally renowned Stanley Thompson in the early 1920s. After moving to the present location in 1970 with a Bob Moote design, its architectural pedigree was further enhanced in 2002, when noted Canadian golf architect Graham Cooke undertook an extensive renovation that perfectly merged a nostalgic feel with a challenging layout that appeals to all abilities. The course ranges in length from 5,350 to over 6,900 yards, but a golfer's ability to finish the last few holes generally determines who will be buying the rounds in the clubhouse.

The final two holes begin with an uphill climb from the 17th tee which, after a long game, can require stamina and mental focus to prepare for the final 1,000 yards. When standing on the 18th tee, the hazards ahead are clear. The right-side fairway bunker is in play, while only the big hitters need to worry about the one on the left. An out-of-bounds along the left side further brings the right side bunker into play.

The second stroke is another uphill shot, and positioning in the fairway is most important. A fairly steep uphill approach with a short iron requires a great deal of trust in club selection, as the prevailing winds and an uphill lie create one of the most difficult shots to control; any ball short and the front bunker will be waiting. Hitting over the green could leave you in a downhill sloping trap. In both cases an up and down becomes a rare feat. Too far from the pin, and a player will have a difficult two-putt for par on this large, sloping green.

Photographs by Nat Caron Photography

BEACH GROVE
Golf & Country Club

The English Tudor-style clubhouse, built in 1929, evokes an era of elegance and welcoming charm that is still the hallmark of Beach Grove Golf & Country Club. The stately, 27,000-square-foot structure, with its massive fireplaces and vaulted ceilings, has always been the focal point for members who enjoy the social interaction and family-oriented camaraderie as much as the superb dining, recreational facilities, and classic golf course. The beautifully treed parkland, with views of Lake St. Clair, provided legendary course architect Stanley Thompson with an ideal setting for one of his true masterpieces. The 6,714-yard layout has hosted numerous top-level championships, yet with four sets of tee boxes is also a delight to play for beginners, juniors, seniors, and all players in between.

Thompson's timeless artistry is on full display at the 7th hole. Playing at 303 yards from the forward tee deck and 362 yards from the back, this beguiling par 4 is all about the tee shot. The 7th gently doglegs around a large pond that skirts the left side of the hole, then curls slightly back to the right. A multi-fingered target bunker on the right side is backed by 10 large Austrian pines atop a burn that runs almost to the green. With a trailing wind, big hitters might try to carry the corner of the pond. The traditional "push up" green, at 7,000 square feet and protected by three bunkers, is one of the largest at Beach Grove. It slopes back to front, making par a real challenge for any approach shots that go long.

Photograph by Glenn Gervais

BEACON HALL
Golf Club

PAR 4 ◆ 434 YARDS

Aurora, ON
905.841.9122
www.beaconhall.com

From both visual and strategic standpoints, the 13th is considered by many to be the most spectacular par 4 at Beacon Hall Golf Club—or anywhere. With remnants of horse jumps off the tee, the property's heritage as the former home to the Toronto and North York Hunt Club is never more present. The 13th is the start of the last six holes, and many a game has been ruined by this daunting stretch of demanding golf, which architect Bob Cupp called very unforgiving to the timid player. By this time in the round, players should be well educated and ready to play or they will pay the price.

From an elevated tee, this tremendous, 434-yard par 4 features probably the most inviting tee shot on the course, visually begging the golfer to really let loose. The left slope is lined with three bunkers, increasingly smaller and deeper the longer the tee shot. In spite of the generous overall width, if the faded tee shot is not played into the area near the bunkers the approach must be made over the lurking pond right of the green. An errant tee shot to the right will find either deep fescue or an area of altered stances that makes even short irons difficult. The approach to the green requires a mid-to-short-iron and the back-right pin, similar to the 9th, is divided by a roll jutting into the putting surface from the steep back slope of the green. An overly cautious shot to the left of the green to avoid the pond will leave golfers with a demanding two-putt. It is a classic hole with enough room off the tee to make everyone comfortable enough to bust it, but from then on in it becomes more and more restricting.

Photograph courtesy of Beacon Hall Golf Club

BIGWIN ISLAND
Golf Club

PAR 4 ◆ 462 YARDS

Lake of Bays, ON
705.635.2582
www.bigwinisland.com

With its soaring cliffs, enchanting inlets, golden sand beaches, and captivating views of the beautiful Lake of Bays in the heart of the summer vacation area of Muskoka, it is little wonder that the luxurious Bigwin Inn became the playground of Hollywood's brightest stars. Where once the rich and famous like the Rockefellers, royalty and dukes—like Ellington—and luminaries like Clark Gable and Carole Lombard partied and played on a course designed by Stanley Thompson, now island cottage owners and visitors play on one of Canada's finest golf courses.

Amongst the towering hardwoods and winding through the undulating island terrain, celebrated architect Doug Carrick created an instant classic, evoking the timeless traditions of a bygone era. The 75 golden silica sand bunkers strategically placed over the 7,166-yard layout, the large gently contoured greens, and the enticing yet challenging landing areas would make Thompson proud.

Carrick's masterful use of Bigwin's natural and rustic beauty is evident on every hole, and nowhere more so than the aptly name Look Out. The tee boxes on the 6th hole afford one of the game's most spectacular views down the dramatic slope, over the forest, and to the glistening lake and a cluster of islands in the distance. Playing from 356 yards back to 462 yards, the four tees allow players to enjoy "hang time" as their shots soar to the fairway 100 feet below. Two bunkers on the left define the landing area, and a large deep trap guards the right side of the large green. The Look Out is as challenging as it is beautiful.

Photograph © Clive Barber

BRAMPTON
Golf Club

PAR 4 ◆ 424 YARDS

Brampton, ON
905.457.4443
www.bramptongolf.com

The last of Brampton Golf Club's triumvirate of scenic and challenging finishing holes, the 18th exemplifies the club's heritage of a classic design executed to modern-day standards. Over the past two decades, the club and course have undergone a multitude of upgrades, renovations, and improvements, all designed to further enhance the golf experience of members and guests. In addition to work on a number of holes, the club added a new halfway house and a spacious new pro shop. In tandem with the various projects, more than 1,000 trees were planted or repositioned.

Many of those trees define the closing hole, a 424-yard par 4—354 yards from the forward tee—that doglegs sharply left as it makes its way to the clubhouse. The Etobicoke Creek Valley and the sidehill of long fescue on the left encourage tee shots to the right center of the fairway. Aggressive attempts to cut the corner must avoid three fairway bunkers at the dogleg. Typical of C.E. "Robbie" Robinson's design, the 18th green is large, measuring 30 yards by 34 yards, and guarded by three sand traps. Two large bunkers are at the front of the green, on the left and right sides; the other is a pot bunker at the back right. The slightly elevated putting surface appears benign, but there is a subtle break toward the Valley. In the early and late parts of the season, the 18th plays into the prevailing northwest wind. During the summer, it plays slightly downwind, putting the onus on club selection off the tee and on second shots on this well-designed finale.

Photograph courtesy of Brampton Golf Club

THE BRIARS
Golf Club

PAR 4 ◆ 399 YARDS

Jackson's Point, ON
905.722.3772
www.briarsgolf.com

Players at The Briars Golf Club, on the south shore of Lake Simcoe just an hour north of Toronto, are treated to a rare sense of the game's history and traditions. The course is challenging but not overwhelming, walkable but not tiresome, intriguing but not confusing, diminutive but not susceptible. Each hole and every fairway, all the bunkers and green complexes, bear the signatures of two masters of golf architecture, Stanley Thompson and C. E. Robinson. The legendary Thompson's nine opened in 1922; the nine by his protégé "Robbie" in 1972. Together they are The Briars Golf Club and have bedevilled the best pros and beguiled amateurs since their openings. Fortunate members own this lush park land by the lake, welcoming their personal guests and golfers staying at The Briars resort.

The 17th hole exemplifies The Briars' timeless design and why members and guests have been returning to it since the Roaring '20s. It plays just under 400 yards from the back tees, just over 300 from the forward of the four tee boxes, and requires careful thought and execution. Players must focus on the tree-lined fairway that doglegs right at almost 90 degrees. The ideal tee shot just past the corner leaves perhaps the most challenging approach shot on the course.

With a mid-iron or hybrid in hand, players look at the narrow opening to the deep green, trying not to think of the pond on the right...or the bunker on the left front...or the Black River winding along the left back of the green. Whatever the outcome of this arduous shot, they will be thinking that Thompson and Robinson were masterful.

Photograph courtesy of The Briars Golf Club

BROCKVILLE
Country Club

16 HOLE

PAR 4 ◆ 389 YARDS

Brockville, ON
613.342.3023
www.brockvillecountryclub.com

Founded in 1914 and redesigned by Stanley Thompson, Brockville Country Club's first impression is that of a traditional course, but an expansion in 1976 and complete renovation have created a premier, year-round golf, curling, and banquet facility for Eastern Ontario.

The course is a shotmaker's course and quite deceptive. Not long by today's standards—6,343 yards from the tips—the par-72, tree-lined course, with its many narrow fairways, requires accuracy off the tees. The greens are fast with plenty of undulation, but are welcoming on approach shots with ample room to land. Patience and precision are a must throughout all 18 holes, so bringing your "A game" is essential. The considerable elevation changes, which occur throughout the course, add to the challenge while offering splendid panoramic views back toward the St. Lawrence River.

The 16th hole is emblematic of the club's interesting and challenging nature. At 389 yards from the back tees, the 90-degree dogleg left requires accuracy and the right club selection to reach the 150 yard marker in order to see the green at the turn. This second shot is played from a raised fairway, over a valley to a large, back-to-front sloping green protected by towering pines and a deep bunker. Four is a good score here. And while trudging up the long hill from the 16th green to the highly elevated 17th tee, players should look back at the wonderful view across the 16th and 3rd fairways, which is indicative of the course's natural setting. The locals are well aware of Brockville Country Club's allure; it's the regional golfers that need to put BCC on their must-play list.

Photographs by Scott MacLeod, www.FlagstickGolfPhotography.com

CAMELOT
Golf and Country Club

18 HOLE

PAR 4 ◆ 448 YARDS

Cumberland, ON
618.833.0801
www.camelotgolf.com

From the stately clubhouse on a high ridge overlooking the Ottawa River, members and their guests at Camelot Golf and Country Club enjoy a view that stretches more than 18 miles down the river valley and out over the picturesque Gatineau Hills. Also in view are nine of the spectacular 18 championship holes designed by award-winning architect Thomas McBroom, the most dramatic being the double green shared by the 9th and 18th holes. The beautiful, natural setting of majestic pines, open spaces, and steep wooded slopes is just 15 minutes outside the nation's capital, Ottawa. Yet since 1991 the equity members have enjoyed a quietude and elegant lifestyle reminiscent of King Arthur's Camelot. The names of the holes—Excalibur, Merlin's Trap, Guinevere, Holy Grail—evoke the club's legendary namesake. Players teeing it up at any of the five tee boxes on the opening hole, First Crusade, know that from 5,171 yards or back at 7,021 yards, Camelot will be more challenging than congenial.

Apropos of a bilingual club, and the fact that Sir Lancelot was French, the 18th at Camelot is named Dernière Croisade. At 448 yards from the back tees, a stout heart is required to leave the green victorious. Rated as the most difficult of the eight par 4s, the tee boxes are positioned 75 feet above the fairway, narrowed by three bunkers on the right of the landing area and dense forest on the left. The undulating fairway then climbs 60 feet to a narrow opening to the green that will repel any short shots back down the slope. The small putting surface is guarded by a large bunker front right, and two more to the right side. Fortunately at Camelot's 18th, even the vanquished are rewarded by a magnificent view of the valley.

Photograph courtesy of Camelot Golf and Country Club

CARLETON
Golf & Yacht Club

PAR 4 ♦ 364 YARDS

Manotick, ON
613.692.3531
www.carletongolf.com

With water on 10 holes, narrow fairways with 12 doglegs, small greens, 60 white silica sand bunkers, and towering trees defining the fairways, Carleton Golf & Yacht Club is a true shotmaker's course. The par-71 layout plays to just over 6,400 yards from the back tees, and 6,100 and 5,600 from the other two, making thoughtful club selection a requisite. Driver is not the automatic choice, even on the par 5s. That the club twice hosted the Canadian Seniors Championship, including 2002 when only three players finished under par, attests to the quality of the design.

Architect Ian Andrew, who works with Masters Champion Mike Weir on course design, is developing a long-range plan to renovate and modernize all 18 holes while maintaining the family orientation of the Carleton club. Learning to shape shots left and right is fundamental to scoring well at Carleton. The 16th is a beautiful dogleg par 4 playing 364 yards from the back tees, 343 yards from the forward set. This may be the most difficult tee shot on the course because it is essential to find the fairway. It is tempting but very dangerous to try and go over the trees on the left, but it is just as challenging to play a full shot down the right and avoid the bunker and trees there. A lay up to the corner is wise, but leaves a long second shot with a large white pine leaning into the line of play near the green. The putting surface is small and nuanced with subtle breaks, with a backdrop of massive white pines right out of a Group of Seven painting. It is the most beautiful setting on the course.

Photograph by Scott MacLeod, www.FlagstickGolfPhotography.com

CASSELVIEW
Golf and Country Club

11 HOLE

PAR 4 ◆ 432 YARDS

Casselman, ON
613.798.4653
www.casselview.com

For more than three decades, the beautiful holes incorporating the naturally undulating terrain, four strategically placed ponds, and the charming Butternut Creek have made Casselview Golf and Country Club a must-play course in the Capital Region. Just a 25-minute drive from Ottawa, the par-72 championship layout is renowned for its superb conditioning and unsurpassed service. The sprawling clubhouse affords panoramic views of the golf course and its groomed fairways that slope and turn, and are accented by streams, mature trees, and ponds. No two holes are alike. The excellent design requires careful club selection from all five sets of tees, and thoughtful approaches to the putting surfaces, some of which are raised while others have false fronts. Whether from the championship tees at 6,705 yards or from the forward tees at 5,330 yards, guests are treated to an immaculately maintained course and an enjoyable, affordable round.

The 11th hole brings all of Casselview's design elements and characteristics into play. The par 4 is a severe dogleg left and all players, from the back tees forward, must be wary of the trees on both sides of the fairway and the bunker on the left corner. Players challenging the dogleg with a tee shot over the bunker must look out for the large pond that borders the last half of the hole on the right. Tucked over on that side and protected by the pond, the long green is a daunting target. A well-placed drive at Casselview's beautiful 11th can be rewarding, but it is not without its risks.

Photograph by Scott MacLeod, www.FlagstickGolfPhotography.com

CHEDOKE CIVIC
Golf Club

18 HOLE

PAR 4 ◆ 430 YARDS

Hamilton, ON
905.546.3116
www.golfhamilton.ca

Chedoke Civic Golf Club's Beddoe Course is set in beautiful mature park land defined by rolling terrain, grand tree-lined fairways, Chedoke Creek, and the ever-present Niagara Escarpment. Originally known as Hamilton Golf Club and renamed Chedoke Civic Golf Club in 1924, the property has been host to the sport of golf since 1896. In 1951, it became the first 36-hole municipal course in Canada.

Not a long course by today's standards, measuring 5,464 from the forward tees and 6,084 from the back, it's easy to assume that a driver is not necessary. But this course has teeth, and playing to a par 70 will challenge the abilities of every level of golfer. With tight landing areas and rolling fairways, small undulating greens make the Beddoe a great test for any golfer's shotmaking skills. The 18th is a demanding par 4 that requires accuracy and length off the tee. Aim your tee shot down the right side of the fairway, as the landing area features a severe right-to-left slope generated by the Escarpment.

On the second shot, hit with a high mid-to-long-iron to reach and stay on this uphill, back-to-front sloping green. Missing the green short should not present any issues, as a "bump and run" should get you in range for par. Avoid being long, as missing this green to the back will require a delicate downhill chip to a putting surface that severely breaks away from the golfer. The Beddoe requires the use of every club in your bag, and the beautiful and challenging 18th will certainly settle a few friendly wagers.

Photograph courtesy of City of Hamilton, Chedoke Civic Golf Club

95

CHERRY HILL
Club

15 HOLE

PAR 4 ◆ 385 YARDS

Ridgeway, ON
905.894.1122
www.cherryhillclub.ca

Changes to hole 15 at Cherry Hill Club have rendered the green visible from the tee, but this hole still sets up as a dogleg left. The pond has been expanded to bring it more into play off the tee, as it sits alongside the final third of the fairway and encroaches on the front of the green. An enlarged water area adds challenge to any attempted long approach from the midpoint of the fairway.

Overplay a shot to avoid the water on the left and two large fairway bunkers wait on the right just over 230 yards out. Another pair of bunkers, in conjunction with the pond, nearly blocks the front of this small green, which slopes severely from back to front. Restricted access and the sloping green make accuracy critical on the approach. It is essential that players account for the slope in relation to pin placement when determining how to play onto the green. Discretion is certainly the better part of valor here.

The hole has proven demanding, even for professionals. From the highlight reel, Gay Brewer chipped in for a par from the back side of the green to maintain his one-shot lead and go on to win the 1972 Canadian Open. In a less auspicious moment, Ray Floyd four-putted number 15 in the 1982 CPGA Championship. No matter how many times you play it, this is one hole that will never become routine.

Photographs by John Gall

COPETOWN WOODS
Golf Club

PAR 4 ♦ 429 YARDS

Copetown, ON
905.627.4653
www.copetownwoods.com

Established in 2003, Copetown Woods Golf Club quickly became one of the region's most popular golf courses, as the terrain of this one-time 200-acre broccoli farm had the exact attributes that course architect Dick Kirkpatrick required to transform it into a fine and rewarding test of golf. The rolling landscape and naturally sandy soil, combined with the existing trees, streams, hills, flora, and fauna, was a perfect canvas for the creation of what is considered one of the best golf values in the entire province. The property is a nature-lover's paradise.

Measuring 6,975 yards, this 18-hole golf course has a links feel to it. Waste bunkers are in abundance, as are some of the largest, most heavily contoured greens in Southwest Ontario, where many a three-putt has occurred. The 9th hole is impressive, measuring 429 yards from the tips and allowing big hitters to let loose off the tee.

From all five sets of tees, the hole seems relatively straightforward: hit it down the middle. The prevailing winds can play havoc with any mishit shot and the tall fescue that lines both sides of the fairway minimize the possibility of reaching the green in regulation should your ball find this danger.

The second shot, should you be on the fairway, makes its way toward the impressive Victorian-style clubhouse that overlooks the putting surface. One of the largest and most challenging greens on the course at nearly 9,000 square feet, this beautifully sculptured green is well guarded by white sand bunkers left and right, so judge the wind, choose the correct club, and a birdie will be your reward.

Photograph courtesy of Copetown Woods Golf Club

CREDIT VALLEY
Golf and Country Club

6 HOLE

PAR 4 ◆ 488 YARDS

Mississauga, ON
905.275.2505
www.creditvalleygolf.com

An original Ojibwa First Nations hunting and fishing ground is now home to one of Ontario's finest private clubs and one of Canada's premier golf facilities. Designed in the 1930s by the legendary Stanley Thompson, who masterfully crafted the original six holes, Credit Valley Golf and Country Club's nine-hole layout was completed in 1934. The '70s saw the course updated by internationally renowned course architect C.E. "Robbie" Robinson, who commented on his first visit that he had never seen a more perfect natural setting for a golf course.

The elevated tee of the 6th hole sits 120 feet above the fairway, making the perfect line for a tee shot just left of center to avoid the fairway bunker on the right and to provide the best angle to the green. A generous landing area may cause overconfidence, but length and accuracy at the number-one handicap hole are a must to set up your second shot for a reasonable attempt at reaching the green in regulation. A hybrid or long-iron from 225 to 175 yards out must carry the Credit River and avoid the two large green side bunkers, which guard this elevated and well-contoured green. Don't be short, as the false front will leave a very difficult chip to a green which slopes from back to front and right to left. Shots left of the flag provide the best opportunity to be aggressive for a birdie or par attempt.

Photograph courtesy of Credit Valley Golf and Country Club

DEERHURST HIGHLANDS

Golf Course at Deerhurst Resort

PAR 4 ◆ 464 YARDS

Huntsville, ON
888.328.1795
www.deerhurstresort.com/golf

The Muskoka Lakes region is world-renowned as one of the game's finest golf destinations. It all started here at the iconic Deerhurst Highlands Golf Course at Deerhurst Resort, the first championship course in Muskoka. The magnificent co-design by two of golf's leading architects, Bob Cupp and Tom McBroom, opened in 1990 and set the area's standard for quality, challenge, and playability for all golfers. The greens average more than 5,000 square feet and 74 well-placed bunkers enhance the layout. With six sets of tee decks, Deerhurst Highlands plays from 5,000 yards to just over 7,000 yards, providing every player with dramatic elevation changes and spectacular views of dense forests, lakes, and granite outcroppings.

The 10th hole is a par 4, playing at 237 yards from the front tee deck to a robust 464 yards from the back tee deck. Players have a wonderful view from the elevated tees of the fairway doglegging left to right. Tall pine trees on the left side of the fairway and a spectacular sheer granite wall on the right frame the 10th. A solid and well-positioned drive past the dogleg is required to reach the green in two shots. The putting surface is large—6,500 square feet—and multi-tiered, but designed to receive well-struck fairway wood and hybrid shots. Cupp and McBroom created a false front and runoff areas beside the green to place a premium on accuracy. Club selection is also critical because of the tiers. Approach shots must land on the proper level for any chance at a birdie; those ending up on the wrong tier create a challenging two-putt. This classic par 4 is a visually stunning and exciting introduction to the back nine at the beautiful Deerhurst Highlands.

Photograph © Clive Barber

DRAGON'S FIRE
Golf Club

PAR 4 ◆ 416 YARDS

Flamborough, ON
905.690.0069
www.dragonsfiregolf.com

On the rolling terrain of a former tree nursery, Dragon's Fire Golf Club rests so naturally on the land that it appears to be decades old. Yet the public club opened in 2008 to, not surprisingly, rave reviews. Set on 198 acres and surrounded by farmland, with some 40 species of trees lining fairways and isolating holes—more than 2,000 trees were moved during construction—Dragon's Fire is a classic park land layout. With no housing or adjacent roadways, each hole on celebrated architect Boris "Bo" Danov's design is cut into its own envelope of towering trees and indigenous flowering shrubbery. No two holes look, or play, alike.

The 6th at Dragon's Fire is a very subtle design, hugged by environmentally protected marshes along the entire right side. It plays to 416 yards from the furthest of the six tee boxes and 291 from the forward-most, calling for an aggressive tee shot to set up a birdie try. From all but the forward tee deck, tee shots easily carry a small pond with the ideal target just short of the fairway bunker on the left. The fairway narrows past the bunker, but there is plenty of room on the right side that is not visible from the tees. Two bunkers protect the right-front of the green that sits diagonally to the fairway and slopes front to back. Because of the angle, the green is shallow and more challenging on second shots from the right side of the landing area. From there, the corner of the woodlot extends almost to the edge of the bunkers and must be carried. Tall trees encircle this naturally secluded green on this beautiful par 4.

Photograph courtesy of Dragon's Fire Golf Club

DRAGON'S FIRE
Golf Club

PAR 4 ◆ 435 YARDS

Flamborough, ON
905.690.0069
www.dragonsfiregolf.com

While the course was under construction, owner Bryan DeCunha opened a website and asked for suggestions on the name—that is how it came to be Dragon's Fire Golf Club. He also asked, "If you were to build your own golf course, what would you like to see?" It was a remarkable, and successful, application of modern social media to the ancient game. DeCunha and architect Boris "Bo" Danov incorporated many ideas from the thousands of responses on size of greens, forced carries, width of fairways, and others into the brilliant design that challenges the finest golfers while catering to the public player. The award-winning result is a layout that measures 7,202 yards from the back tees, has no forced carries from the three forward-most tees thanks to six tee deck options, offers generous landing areas for higher handicap players, is easily walked, and can be enjoyed by all golfers, from pros to beginners.

The elevated tees on the 11th hole provide a wonderful view of the deeply wooded landscape that creates full separation of the holes. A wide variety of tree species line and define the fairway and hint at the gentle dogleg on this mid-length par 4. The dogleg and narrowness of the green puts a premium on the tee shot. Three fairway bunkers, two on the left, direct players to the point the fairway starts down the hill. The ideal drive is a power fade to catch the down slope that can leave just a wedge approach. Tee shots that stay on top require a mid-iron to a shallow green tucked slightly to the right and guarded by bunkers front and back. The 11th offers a good opportunity for birdie, but approach shots that carry long can make a score of par a moral victory.

Photographs courtesy of Dragon's Fire Golf Club

EAGLES NEST
Golf Club

12 HOLE

PAR 4 ◆ 470 YARDS

Maple, ON
905.417.2300
www.eaglesnestgolf.com

The great Bobby Jones once said, "Only a really good course will afford you the opportunity to use every club in the bag." With that said, welcome to Eagles Nest Golf Club. An exquisite balance of nature and design, Eagles Nest has been recognized as one of the best public golf courses in the country.

The 12th, known as Macallan and jokingly named for the best 12-year-old scotch in the world, has an elevated tee which not only showcases the magnificence of the golf course but brings a sense of freedom following the tough opening holes of the back nine. At 470 yards from the Eagle tees, players hope the prevailing wind is at hand.

From the high perch, players must hit a tee shot that navigates the spectacle of bunkers guarding the inside of the fairway. If successfully challenged, golfers will be rewarded by finding a sloped fairway that propels balls forward, setting up a short iron to the green. The fairway is far from level, and calculating the wind direction and finding a flat lie to execute your second shot can be precarious. Your approach must be precise, as the green measures only 27 yards in depth and slopes significantly from back to front. The back-right pin position is the most devious, as it is protected by a small pot bunker short and a closely mown area long and right of the green site. When finished, think about having a "wee dram" to celebrate your success on this hole.

Photograph © Clive Barber

ELMIRA
Golf Club

16 HOLE

PAR 4 ◆ 429 YARDS

Elmira, ON
519.669.1652
www.elmiragolfclub.com

Golfers visiting the challenging and enjoyable Elmira Golf Club in the scenic farming area west of Toronto are surprised to learn that the beautiful course was designed and built by members and volunteers. The layout has all the nuances, elevation changes, bunkering, treed corridors, mounding, and subtle greens of layouts designed by signature architects. However, few such courses have the inherent charm of Elmira, born of that volunteer determination and community spirit.

Set on 145 rolling acres, Elmira is also unique for its configuration of 12 par 4s, to go with four par 3s and just two par 5s, one on each side. The only professional design touch is David Moote's reshaping of the 10th and 11th holes and addition of some bunkers in the early 1990s. At more than 6,300 yards from the back tees and 5,185 yards from the forward tees, Elmira is a good walk, enhanced.

One of Elmira's finest par 4s is the 16th, which incorporates many of the layout's enduring characteristics. The tree-lined tee shot is straight uphill, with Larches Creek crossing in front of the two back tees. Playing longer than its distance on the card—429 yards from the blacks, 314 yards from the reds—the 16th doglegs slightly right after cresting the steep hill. This hole demands a good tee shot as the fairway slopes left to right, making the ideal landing position left of center. The second shot into the 27-yard-deep, back-to-front sloping green—no bunkers are required, the approach is challenging enough—must carry Larches Creek, which winds its way across the entire front of the green, and the statuesque tree on the right just short of the putting surface. The 16th offers risks, and the occasional reward.

Photographs courtesy of Elmira Golf Club

eQUINELLE
Golf Club

PAR 4 ◆ 405 YARDS

Kemptville, ON
613.258.2105
www.eQuinelleGolf.ca

The historic town of Kemptville, just outside the nation's capital of Ottawa, provides the ideal landscape for recreation, rural living with urban access, and spectacular golf. Within the master-planned golf course community of eQuinelle Golf Club, there is a perfect combination of golf plus town and country living. With a résumé that includes celebrated golf courses such as Le Maître at Mont Tremblant and Le Fontainebleau, Darrell Huxham of Huxham Golf Designs created eQuinelle Golf Club to challenge and delight residents and guests, whether beginners or scratch players. Huxham blended large bunkers and indigenous fescue grasses with bentgrass fairways, greens, and tees into a 7,100-yard, par-72 championship test.

The par-4 5th hole is a fine example of Huxham's subtle park land and links-style design. It follows the arduously long 604-yard 4th, and at first glance might appear to be a respite. But incorporating all the elements of the links portion of Huxham's layout, this beautiful hole plays straightaway with fescue bordering the fairway on both the right and left. While the landing area is generous, there is a bunker complex on the left and the prevailing wind is right to left. A tee shot down the right-hand side of the fairway will avoid trouble and leave an easier approach to the large but protected green. Longer hitters beware: The fairway narrows significantly just past the landing area, with a bunker complex on the right. All approach shots should be carefully played, as the fast-running green slopes to collection areas front-right and back-left. And the deep pot bunker at the front left of the green can spell disaster. Welcome to the National Capital Region's newest championship golfing experience, proudly managed by TMSI Sports Management.

Photograph by Betty Cooper

HAMILTON
Golf & Country Club

PAR 4 ◆ 446 YARDS

Ancaster, ON
905.648.4471
www.hgcc.ca

There are few holes in golf that challenge players from the tee as much as they do into the green. This is what makes the 9th hole on the south course at Hamilton Golf & Country Club such a great hole, as golfers play into one of the most spectacular, elevated amphitheater greens in golf. Hamilton is one of 10 founding clubs of the Royal Canadian Golf Association—now Golf Canada—with a history dating back to 1894. Today's magnificent layout by none other than famed English golf course architect Harry S. Colt opened on June 1, 1916. Since that time, the club has hosted numerous amateur and professional championships, including five Canadian Opens.

The best way to play the 9th is to hit a fairway wood or long-iron down the left side and hopefully roll the ball to the bottom of the slope. If you leave the ball short on the slope, it's tough to hit the uphill second shot off a downhill lie. From the right edge of the fairway, it's a difficult angle to approach the green. The second shot must be crisp, since it plays very long up the hill. Usually it's tough to get the ball pin high, but that's okay—the green is very severe from back to front and putting is much easier from short of the hole.

Photograph by Grant Fraser

IDYLWYLDE
Golf & Country Club

PAR 4 ◆ 400 YARDS

Sudbury, ON
705.522.8580
www.idylwylde.com

Since 1922, the idyllic, undulating terrain between Lakes Ramsey and Nepahwin near the heart of Sudbury has been home to Idylwylde Golf & Country Club. Set among stands of birch and coniferous trees and punctuated by rocky outcrops, the 6,594-yard layout's narrow, rolling fairways, small and sloping greens, beautiful lake views, and well-placed bunkers make it one of Northern Ontario's finest courses. Idylwylde is a shotmaker's delight, but with four sets of tees it is welcoming to all players, as it plays to 5,244 yards from the forward tees. The only private golf club in Sudbury, Idywylde also has its own private beach on the peninsula, and the curling club is the home of champions.

The beautiful shoreline of Lake Nepahwin frames three holes on the back nine: 10, 12, and 13. From the tee box at the par-4 13th, players look out over the diagonal fairway,

the lake with its backdrop of rock cliffs, and Laurentian Beach. From the back tees, the hole plays 400 yards, with the lake on the right and a birch forest on the left. The bold aim tee shots over the corner of the lake, while the conservative play it down the left where the fairway widens. All second shots are challenging, as the tiered green is a full 50 feet above the fairway at the top of "cardiac hill," the steepest elevation change on the course. The climb reveals the very deep bunker protecting the front left of the green and the long, narrow one at the back. Any players managing a two-putt on this sloping and treacherous green can catch their breath and look back down the fairway to enjoy one of the finest views on the course.

Photograph by Jay Sisko

ISLINGTON
Golf Club

1st HOLE

PAR 4 ◆ 368 YARDS

Islington, ON
416.231.1114
www.islingtongolfclub.com

When Islington Golf Club co-hosted the 2010 RBC Canadian Open, the opening hole was transformed into a world-class practice facility for PGA Tour professionals. It was a sight to behold, as the likes of John Daly, Mike Weir, Fred Couples, Tim Clark, Luke Donald, eventual winner Carl Pettersson, and others warmed up before their round.

Now the 1st hole at Islington is a 368-yard par 4 that eases members and guests into the round. Standing on the first tee, golfers are captivated by the towering silver maple trees that line both sides of the lush, rambling fairway. There are no bunkers to contend with until golfers reach the green—only thick rough that can make for a challenging second shot—and players definitely don't want to find themselves behind one of the many trees.

At the green, golfers are greeted by the first of a series of classic bunkers, which dot the Islington landscape and give the course its teeth. They were originally designed by legendary Canadian golf course architect Stanley Thompson and masterfully restored by Carrick Design. There's a deceptively large entrance to the green guarded by perilous bunkers at each corner, but when the pin is at the back a two-putt is a good score and a three-putt is the reality for many. Thompson, a true master of Canadian golf course design, has created a very walkable park land layout at Islington, and the 1st is the gateway to what is considered a Canadian classic that has stood the test of time for 90 years.

Photographs: above by Chris Bacik, facing page © Clive Barber

ISLINGTON
Golf Club

PAR 4 ◆ 382 YARDS

Islington, ON
416.231.1114
www.islingtongolfclub.com

The game of golf is sometimes described as a walk in the park, and at Islington Golf Club that's especially fitting. As members and guests walk through the picturesque Mimico Creek River valley, there is plenty of spectacular natural beauty just waiting to be explored as golfers indulge their passion for the game.

Standing on the 7th tee, the flag pole with the Maple Leaf flying is visible adjacent to the elegant clubhouse that was refurbished in 2011. While the 7th is a favorite for many members, it is also a difficult hole for most. The tee shot is intimidating, presenting a hazard and large bunker on the right side, a line of trees to the left, and a narrowing fairway throughout the hole that affects the longer hitters. The preference most days is to land the ball middle to right of the fairway for the best shot to the green.

For the second shot, golfers have to deal with hazards all down the right side, including a wonderful Stanley Thompson bunker with a small grass island in the center of it, just to the left of the green. It's wiser to take a peek at it while you're walking by than having to play a shot out of it. As with a number of holes at Islington, the green has some hard-to-read undulations and slopes, particularly from back to front. The green is narrow in front and widens to the back and there's a false front that golfers need to be wary of—there's really no room for error, and golfers definitely do not want to hit the approach shot beyond the hole.

Photographs: above by Chris Bacik, facing page © Clive Barber

KING'S FOREST
Golf Club

PAR 4 ◆ 395 YARDS

Hamilton, ON
905.546.4781
www.golfhamilton.ca

King's Forest Golf Club features many wonderful holes, but all golfers should experience the challenge of its par-4 11th. With a tee box that practically sits in the treetops, golfers are faced with a well-manicured, tree-lined fairway 100 feet below. A confident tee shot is a must, as downhill drives can be difficult in perceiving distance and direction. The ideal position on 11 will be left-center to create the best angle for reaching the green. Any errant shot—left or right—and the trees will most certainly come into play.

To reach this medium-sized green that is encircled by the trees of King's Forest, the second shot from the fairway requires accuracy to avoid the small pond fronting the green and the periphery of the long, shaggy grass along its banks. A menacing bunker that is visible from the tee box and a small pond stand guard along the right of the green, ready to capture any wayward approach shots.

The green plays true, and a one-putt is often the reward if the ball is positioned below the cup. Those who make it past this par 4 will feel a great sense of exhilaration, since playing this beautiful and taxing golf hole is challenge enough, but scoring par or better is a true triumph.

Photographs courtesy of City of Hamilton, King's Forest Golf Club

LOCH MARCH
Golf & Country Club

PAR 4 ◆ 435 YARDS

Kanata, ON
613.839.5885
www.lochmarch.com

The Canadian Shield is as rugged as it is beautiful, and can be treacherous for those not sure of their step. For two years, Mark Fuller walked his 300 acres of rock, forest, and swamp 25 minutes west of Ottawa's Parliament Buildings. An admirer of the legendary Canadian architect Geoffrey Cornish, Fuller—with a background in heavy construction and property management—walked the dense woods mindful of Cornish's philosophy, refined by years working with the great Stanley Thompson, of finding the golf holes rather than imposing them on the land. Fuller eventually found beautiful fairways, ideal locations for greens, natural hazards, and contours in the heavily treed slopes. He measured potential golf shots by threading fishing line from his cut-down fishing rod—color-coded line for every ten yards—to calibrate landing areas, pinpoint doglegs, and measure the lengths of possible holes. Gradually he put the puzzle together. After two years of construction under the watchful eye of superintendent Sid Witteveen, Loch March Golf & Country Club opened in 1987.

The attempt begins at the opening hole, one of the toughest on the course and considered one of the most demanding opening holes in the entire Ottawa Valley. From the five elevated tees, players are immediately aware of the water all along the right side that curls in to narrow the fairway. From the back tees at 435 yards, it is only a little more than 200 yards to the water; driver is risky. A conservative play—a mid-iron or hybrid—off the tee, down the left side is rewarded with a comfortable lay up and pitch into a tiered green with large bunkers front and back-left, water right and back. As this is the number-one handicap hole, on most days, for most players, bogey is a great start.

Photograph by Michelle Valberg

LONDON HUNT
and Country Club

PAR 4 ◆ 401 YARDS

London, ON
519.471.6430
www.londonhuntclub.com

Legendary architect Robert Trent Jones is renowned for many characteristics of his award-winning course designs. One of the most enduring is the short par 4. At the prestigious London Hunt and Country Club in southern Ontario, the 14th hole is a classic example. From each of the four tee boxes—ranging from 299 yards to 401 yards—players can fully experience the strategic challenges.

Jones created the London Hunt course in 1959. His son Rees renovated the layout in 1999, staying true to his father's masterful blueprint. At the tee on 14, players must decide whether to lay up on the fairway's upper level or try to carry their shot to the down slope and reach the lower, or second, fairway. The conservative play off the tee to the 32-yard-wide landing area leaves a second shot of about 160 yards to the green with the benefit of a level lie. Aggressive tee shots can have a second shot of 100 yards of less, but from a downhill lie. Only drives from the back tee of 300 yards or more are rewarded with a level lie.

The opening to the large green, with the majestic red brick clubhouse in the background, is defined by trademark Jones bunkers. Tucked up against a large mound, the scallops of a bunker guard the left edge of the putting surface. A deep, massive bunker stretches from the narrow opening almost across the entire front of the green, aided by a tall spruce at the midway point guarding the right side. The 14th at London Hunt is eloquent proof that length does not define the strength of a well-designed hole.

Photograph by Nicole Osborne, NEO Image Creations

THE MAD RIVER
Golf Club

PAR 4 ◆ 461 YARDS

Creemore, ON
705.428.3673
www.madriver.ca

For the members of The Mad River Golf Club, the golfing experience is defined by perennial enjoyment of the landscape's natural features, the varied demands of strategy and shot-making, and the striking aesthetics of the course. And while every hole designed by architect Bob Cupp offers a stimulating mix of these qualities, none showcases them better than the 461-yard 9th hole.

From a slightly elevated tee, the drive plays over the fairway horizon to an unseen landing area, with the hole framed by a thick stand of mature pines on the right and penal fescue on the left. A long drive favoring the right side is essential to find relatively level ground. Even with the first shot ideally placed, the long carry over the pond on the second requires precise club selection and confident execution. To Mad River members, this is one of the great approach shots in golf; successfully executed, it never fails to satisfy.

Reaching the green in regulation is no guarantee of an easy, two-putt par. The putting surface—the largest on the course at 14,000 square feet—is divided into numerous pin positions by a series of small, almost imperceptible mounds and "noses" that extend into the green. Along the pond, falloffs and a deep swale add to challenge of a back-left pin position. Whether putting or chipping, these features can make for some very long and complex rolls, as well as some good fun for those watching from the clubhouse veranda that overlooks the green.

Photograph by Hilton Tudhope

MAPLE CITY
Country Club

PAR 4 ◆ 405 YARDS

Chatham, ON
519.354.8172
www.maplecitycc.com

Nestled amid some of the finest farmland in Southern Ontario, along the winding Thames River just east of Chatham, the ideal tract of land for a challenging golf course was selected by the founding members of Maple City Country Club. In 1957, acclaimed architect C. E. "Robbie" Robinson used this natural topography to create a spectacular layout bordered on two sides by the Thames. The course plays from four sets of tees, ranging from 4,550 yards to 6,612 yards, and features gentle, rolling fairways, valleys throughout, and a natural oxbow of the Thames that runs along and through several holes. Robinson artfully designed the course to be a pleasure for players of all skill levels and a test of the game's best. The site of three provincial championships and a national championship, Maple City also hosted the 2014 Ontario Junior Girls Championship.

The 2nd hole is the number-one handicap hole on the scorecard, and challenges all players right from the tee boxes. The picturesque oxbow of the Thames is an intimidating water hazard that stretches in front of the tee, along the left side of the hole, and then curls back across the approach to the green. The fairway is severely contoured into almost a boomerang shape from tee to green, and slopes to the left from the trees lining the right side. Players hoping for a shorter second shot must risk carrying tall, robust trees about 200 yards out on the left side. From the ideal landing area, players face a 150-yard shot to a green sloped back to front. The ponds in front and the hillside in back of the green provide a beautiful backdrop to Maple City's signature hole.

Photograph by Dan Kosik

MARKLAND WOOD

Golf Club

PAR 4 ◆ 355 YARDS

Etobicoke, ON
416.621.3400
www.marklandwood.com

Considered one of the friendliest and most social of the many fine private golf clubs in the Greater Toronto region, the 18-hole Markland Wood Golf Club is a course that was meant for walking while enjoying the beautiful, tranquil scenery. New members and guests are often amazed that such a serene location is so close to the hustle of nearby Toronto and its international airport.

The course, though not long at 6,259 yards, requires strategy and accuracy; many golfers look at the yardage and expect a driver and a short iron will provide ample opportunities for par or better. This is not the case, as it plays much longer than the yardage suggests due to its lush conditioning. The beauty of Markland Wood can quickly become hazardous, as strategically placed sand traps, subtle breaks in the greens, coniferous trees that line many of the fairways, and Etobicoke Creek—which is a feature on 13 of the holes—are serene in nature but can prove costly with poor shot execution.

The par-4 13th exemplifies both the beauty and the beast of the course from any of the five tee locations. As a medium-length hole, it requires a precise drive. Hit it through the fairway and you're in the water. Too short, and you're blocked out from going at the green. A good drive will leave a short to medium-length iron over water to an elevated green. The false front adds to the excitement of the approach, where a second shot short can leave a difficult chip shot back up the hill. The well-positioned bunkers guarding the putting surface must also be avoided, as many a misjudged shot will find the sand and require a subtle escape to keep the ball below the hole on this fast and sloping green. Accuracy and distance control are a must to create a birdie opportunity.

Photograph by Chris Melidoniotis

MILL RUN
Golf Club

PAR 4 ◆ 402 YARDS

Uxbridge, ON
800.465.8633
www.golfmillrun.com

Built on the highest section of terrain, The Grind nine at Mill Run Golf Club features countless opportunities to experience the beautiful variety of landscapes throughout the property. Alongside The Grist and The Wheel nines, The Grind completes the 27 championship holes at Mill Run. For a wonderful and challenging change of pace, The Highland Course, with its naturally rolling terrain and elevation changes, offers one of the best executive golf course experiences in Ontario. Rounding out the offerings at Mill Run is a practice facility complete with chipping and putting greens, a practice range featuring an expansive bentgrass tee deck, and a talented staff of PGA of Canada Golf Professionals with a passion for teaching the game.

One of the most captivating viewpoints at Mill Run is the tee box on The Grind's 8th hole. At 1,121 feet above sea level—the highest elevation at Mill Run—the dogleg par 4 and the surrounding countryside are in full view. All four tees, stretching the hole from 293 yards back to 402 yards, are set in a narrow chute of trees. A fairway bunker on the left encourages tee shots down the right side. Ideal shots reach the top of the hill, where the hole doglegs right for a great view of the green and the rest of the course.

The green, which from the hill almost appears to be suspended in mid-air, is nicely bunkered and slopes slightly from back to front. Approach shots should favor the front-left of the putting surface. Shots that carry too far are in danger of tumbling down the 50-foot slope behind the green, never to be seen again.

Photograph by Stuart Brindle

MISSISSAUGUA
Golf and Country Club

9 HOLE

PAR 4 ◆ 441 YARDS

Mississauga, ON
905.278.4857
www.mississauguagolf.com

Mississaugua Golf and Country Club is on a site first visited by Governor Sir John Simcoe in 1793. When he and his party paddled up the Credit River, the scene that spread out before them was very different from what it is today. Instead of the magnificent clubhouse surrounded by picturesque fairways and greens, the governor and his men saw a native village. The club's name perpetuates that roving band: the Mississauga, a branch of the great Ojibway nation.

This is where you find the 9th hole, a sensational par 4 that plays from tee to green along the Credit River shoreline. Percy Barrett, George Cumming, and Stanley Thompson each played a significant role in creating the layout we know today. From the tee, which sits on the water's edge, it's an angled shot to the fairway. Standing on the tee, you have to calculate how much of the river you want to bite off and then commit to the shot—it's not for the faint of heart.

The fairway narrows for the second shot with a single bunker at the front-left corner of the green, which slopes quite severely from back to front. The club is also home to outstanding curling and tennis facilities, making it one of the most exceptional country clubs in Canada.

Photograph © Clive Barber

MUSKOKA BAY
Club

PAR 4 ◆ 441 YARDS

Gravenhurst, ON
705.687.7900
www.muskokabayclub.com

When celebrated architect Doug Carrick and developer Peter Freed first walked this rugged Canadian Shield terrain, they knew instinctively that the golf course would start and end on a stunning 100-foot granite cliff at the heart of the property. That precipice is now the site of Muskoka Bay Club's spectacular 17,000-square-foot Clifftop Clubhouse. The clubhouse provides a mix of old Muskoka grandeur combined with modern amenities, complete with casual and fine dining, fitness facilities, steam rooms, spa, tennis, and the spectacular clifftop infinity pool overlooking the opening hole. With the panoramic view of the rock outcrops, mixed forest, lakes, ponds, and streams that comprise the unrelenting beauty unique to the Muskokas region, the granite cliff is also the site of the first tee at one of Canada's finest golf courses.

Muskoka Bay opened in 2007 and was immediately recognized by *Golf Digest* and *SCOREGolf* magazines as the best new course in Canada. More telling is that in 2012, *Golfweek Magazine* named Muskoka Bay, in just its fifth year of maturation, as the fifth best modern course in Canada built since 1960. High praise, but as each golfer lucky enough to play the course acknowledges, well deserved.

Appropriately named Table Rock, the opening par-4 1st hole launches players into their round from the granite cliff. The dramatic tee shot to the rolling fairway far below can be made beside markers reading from the Tour 441 yards to the forward 257 yards. Carrick's five tee choices on every hole invite golfers of all ages and abilities to appreciate and enjoy Muskoka Bay. The gentle dogleg right is framed by century-old pines, a beaver meadow, and Carrick's well-placed bunkers. Thoughtful too is his open run-up to the green, encouraged by large sand traps on both sides of the elongated green. Subtle contours of the putting surface cap a welcoming introduction to Muskoka Bay.

Photograph by Peter Wong

MUSKOKA BAY
Club

PAR 4 ◆ 349 YARDS

Gravenhurst, ON
705.687.7900
www.muskokabayclub.com

Over the centuries, many of the holes on golf's most storied courses acquire nicknames that reflect their character and challenges. Architect Doug Carrick, whether tramping links dunes in Scotland or granite outcrops 90 minutes north of Toronto, as he did at Muskoka Bay Club, is never more than a step away from the game's roots. Therefore, it is not surprising that the masterfully crafted holes on his award-winning Muskoka Bay Club have their own distinctive and evocative names.

Nothing is lost in translation for players reading the scorecard at Muskoka Bay. The Tour tees play to a daunting 7,367 yards, and marking down from the championship at 6,849 yards, member/guest at 6,325 yards, middle at 5,703 yards, and forward at 4,981 yards, there are tee options suiting every game. The names of the holes are also helpful. As Muskoka Bay winds through its dramatic descent into the valley, with exposed rock, verdant forest, ponds, and streams, descriptive hole names became part of the experience. Among them is Son of a Birch, Purgatory, Waterloo,

and the benignly named 18th, Home. However, to get home everyone has to play Shorty.

The 4th earned its nickname as the shortest par 4 on the course—349 yards from the Tour tees; 213 yards from the forward tees—but it is no gimme par. The hole plays from an elevated perch of granite left behind by the retreat of the glaciers. Looking down from the tee decks, players will see the tops of the towering 60-foot hardwoods lining the narrow fairway. From all five tee decks, the majestic hardwoods are inspiring but can disguise the wind that can swing tee shots 10 to 15 yards right to left as they carry the hole's dramatic descent. Carrick says the 4th is designed as a heroic downhill short par 4 that can be reached with a long, straight tee shot.

Photograph by Peter Wong

MUSKOKA BAY
Club

PAR 4 ◆ 423 YARDS

Gravenhurst, ON
705.687.7900
www.muskokabayclub.com

Perched on a massive granite cliff, the magnificent clubhouse at Muskoka Bay Club alone is worth the scenic 90-minute drive north from Toronto. From the clubhouse's elevated vantage point, holes 1, 2, 3, and 18 on the award-winning Doug Carrick-designed golf course come into view. So too does the 9th hole as it climbs up the slope between its own dramatic rock formations. Muskoka Bay Club is also the epitome of a Lifestyle Muskoka Oasis. With an array of beautiful homes, villas, and lofts, Muskoka Bay Club offers an experience to fit discerning tastes. The luxurious Stay and Play program for overnight visits allows guests to glimpse the lifestyle opportunities Muskoka Bay Club has to offer.

The 423-yard 9th hole is very aptly called The Narrows for the bold pinching of the fairway by massive exposures of distinctive Canadian Shield granite. The par 4 has also been called "daring architecture" and "unlike any other hole in the world." That is the sentiment shared by players standing on the elevated tee boxes when they look down at the challenges Carrick has sculpted for them. First there is the wetland to carry to reach the fairway that, like the majority at Muskoka Bay, is undulating. Secondly, likely from an uneven lie, players must thread their approach through or over the narrow opening between the massive outcrops, posing like sentinels guarding the green. Mercifully, with sufficient drama in the first two shots, Carrick saw no need for bunkers and created a receptive, bowl-shaped green. As golfers walk up to the clubhouse after playing just the opening nine, they can appreciate why Muskoka Bay has won so many awards and is rated by *SCOREGolf* as among the top 10 golf courses in Canada.

Photograph by Peter Wong

THE NATIONAL
Golf Club of Canada

PAR 4 ◆ 460 YARDS

Woodbridge, ON
416.798.4900
www.nationalgolf.ca

The National Golf Club of Canada was founded in 1974 with only one objective in mind: to be the finest course in Canada. That objective has been achieved, as The National is consistently ranked at or near the top of all courses in Canada. *GOLF Magazine* places The National in the top 100 courses in the world, further confirmation that designers Tom Fazio and his uncle, the late George Fazio, met the original mandate and that the club has held steadily to its objective. With 18 distinctly different holes, The National takes golfers on a challenging tour through upland and lowland, ravine land, and woodland. World Golf Hall of Famer Lee Trevino has said that any tournament played at The National with U.S. Open conditions would be one of the toughest courses to play, certainly holding its own among the great courses in the U.S.

The closing hole epitomizes The National's style: demanding. Playing from 365 yards to 460 yards, the 18th is so challenging that for a period of 15 years it was played as a par 5 by the members. The hole was changed back to a par 4 in 2000, as originally designed, and ever since has been the finale of one of the greatest back-to-back par-4 finishes anywhere. The tee shot is elevated, revealing a spectacular view. The second shot is considerably uphill to an extremely narrow opening and a very small putting surface. To hold this green, approach shots must be high, floating, and accurate—trademark requirements at The National Golf Club of Canada.

Photograph courtesy of The National Golf Club of Canada

OAK BAY
Golf & Country Club

PAR 4 ◆ 342 YARDS

Port Severn, ON
705.538.0893
www.oakbaygolf.com

Complementing one of the most picturesque settings in Canada, Oak Bay Golf & Country Club was nominated as the best new golf course in Canada in 2012. The 6,503-yard layout takes golfers on a remarkable meander through woodlands and along the eastern shoreline of Georgian Bay. Carefully created in a pristine and environmentally sensitive area, with four sets of tee boxes and playing from 4,825 yards from the forward tees to 6,503 yards from the championship tees, Oak Bay is as welcoming as it is beautiful for golfers of all ages.

Views of Georgian Bay and the unique eastern shore topography are constant companions during a round at Oak Bay. And perhaps the finest vantage point is the 7th tee, the highest point of the golf course. From here players have to be reminded why they arrived at this magnificent spot—not to sightsee or look out over the 3rd and 6th holes, but to play a terrific short par 4. The 7th is a great risk/reward hole: hit driver to a very narrow landing area in hopes of a short approach and easy birdie; miss the landing area and hope for bogey.

An iron off the tee to the welcoming layup area is the other option, but neither shot is automatic. The 7th plunges downhill with trees lining both sides of the slight dogleg left, with a fairway bunker looming on the right side. A massive rock outcrop framing the left side of the hole gets everyone's attention. The deep, narrow green sits above the fairway, protected by a large bunker front right and another smaller one back right. Oak Bay's 7th hole has added a third element to risk and reward: beauty.

Photograph by Amy Lepp

THE OAKVILLE
Golf Club

PAR 4 ◆ 340 YARDS

Oakville, ON
905.845.8321
www.oakvillegolfclub.com

Established in 1921, The Oakville Golf Club is a private, nine-hole gem and one of the oldest clubs in the Greater Toronto region. The course has been modernized, but upon entering the tree-lined roadway the old-style ambience and charm is very much in evidence. This is a place where the likes of Bobby Jones and Walter Hagen would have acknowledged the wonder of playing a course so reminiscent of the grand courses where they enjoyed so much professional success.

The course features many narrow fairways, saucer-shaped greens, and just enough trees lining the fairways that the strong east winds blowing from nearby Lake Ontario can create club selection concerns. It can be difficult to hit and hold a shot on these bentgrass greens. A perfect example of the strategy required to play many of the holes at Oakville is the recently redesigned signature hole, the 340-yard, par-4 6th.

While standing on the tee, golfers have to judge their club selection correctly in order to traverse a large pond that fronts the tee box. Next they must execute a carry of 200 yards to find the flat surface of the fairway that will provide the best position to approach the elevated green. An errant shot or one hit over 220 yards, and golfers will have the prospect of searching for their ball in the valley's creek, which runs across the entire width of the fairway, a short distance in front of the green. A well-positioned ball will leave a 120-yard approach shot and miss the water hazard to leave a short-iron to the elevated putting surface. Avoid the large bunker along the right front of this small and undulating green, be cognizant of the wind, putt well, and a birdie will be your reward.

Photograph © Clive Barber

RIDEAU VIEW
Golf Club

PAR 4 ◆ 420 YARDS

Manotick, ON
613.692.3442
www.rideauview.com

The historic Rideau Canal was constructed in 1832 on the assumption of an upcoming war with the United States, and now this scenic waterway is the backdrop for the beautiful Rideau View Golf Club. Considered one of the finest private golf clubs in the region and ranked number 81 in Canada, Rideau View's full 18 holes were completed in 1963 and are a pleasure to play for every level of golfer. A choice of six tee boxes, magnificently manicured fairways, mature trees, and strategically placed bunkers identify Rideau View as a masterpiece of renowned golf course architects Howard Watson and C. E. Robinson.

The 14th is a bonafide championship hole: golfers must manage the prevailing tailwinds and execute a drive that is both accurate and long to find the left side of the fairway and capture the slope, which will roll the ball toward the center. A ball hit too far right meets two large bunkers and a stand of trees, minimizing the opportunity of reaching the green in regulation. A good drive leaves the player with a downwind approach shot with a premium on club selection. The elevated green, only 28 paces across at its widest, could result in the ball rolling off the false front, leaving a very tricky short pitch back up the slope.

A creek meanders across the fairway 80 to 90 yards in front of the green, but don't worry—it's just another harmonizing visual on this beautiful yet challenging hole.

Photographs: above by Matt Wallace; facing page by Brent Long, Better Golf Communications

ROSELAND
Golf and Curling Club

PAR 4 ◆ 467 YARDS

Windsor, ON
519.969.3810
www.citywindsor.ca

Jack Nicklaus once described Donald Ross as the "Michelangelo of golf...he designed courses that led to positive thinking." The championship layout of Roseland Golf and Curling Club, designed by Ross in 1926, captures the essence of the landscape and why we play the game. In 2011, Roseland went through a major restoration by international golf course architects Albanese & Lutzke that modernized and revitalized the 18 holes. It improved the playability for all levels of golfers while preserving the sense of tradition and fair play established by Ross. Owned by the City of Windsor, the course was selected as the host for the 2012 PGA Tour of Canada's Windsor Roseland Charitable Classic event.

The course measures 6,943 yards from the back tees and features many signature holes, including the par-4 18th that epitomizes the course's beauty and challenge. From the recently reworked back tee, which still retains Ross' aesthetics, the strategy is to drive the ball as close as possible to the bunker on the left side of the fairway. This creates the optimal angle to reach the narrow and rolling green and the best opportunity to avoid the two strategically placed greenside bunkers. Play a ball to far right and a green in regulation is almost out of the question, as this tree-lined, 467-yard hole—from the back tees—will require a perfectly hit fairway wood to have any chance at reaching the putting surface. During those warm summer days, the drier conditions and prevailing downwind dramatically decrease the percentage to hold the surface of this undulating and oval-shaped green with any long-iron or wood. Enjoy the experience of a great Donald Ross-inspired finishing hole, a masterpiece to contemplate after the round is over.

Photograph courtesy of Roseland Golf and Curling Club

SILVER LAKES
Golf & Conference Centre

12 HOLE

PAR 4 ◆ 450 YARDS

East Gwillimbury, ON
800.465.7888
www.silverlakesgolf.com

With its bentgrass fairways and manicured greens, Silver Lakes Golf & Conference Centre is often characterized as a true hidden gem of Ontario. Hit long and straight on the 12th hole, as it is not just about accuracy but length. At 450 yards from the back gold tees, this hole is the longest par 4 at Silver Lakes and one of the longest in the entire province. In addition to being the most difficult hole on the back nine on which to make par, the added complexity of constant headwinds make golfers feel as if they need to hit driver to have a reasonable opportunity of getting onto the green in regulation.

The strategy is not to hit it hard, as the fairway is receptive for a slight mishit, but instead to employ an overly aggressive swing. The procession of large trees, from tee box to the distant green, will be your resting place and a recovery shot a necessity.

Having landed in the fairway, the approach shot must be hit down the middle—as long grass on the left and right make getting out awkward—to avoid the two deep bunkers that protect this manicured putting surface. With a forward pin position, a well-placed shot with minimal forward spin will be required to avoid facing a long and treacherous downhill putt on this narrow and back-to-front sloping green. A golfer's talent to read the contours and speed of the putting surface will reduce the likelihood of a three-putt. Securing par will raise the confidence of any player.

Photograph courtesy of Silver Lakes Golf & Conferene Centre

ST. GEORGE'S
Golf and Country Club

PAR 4 ◆ 467 YARDS

Toronto, ON
www.stgeorges.org

With the landmark clubhouse in clear sight behind the green, the essence of St. George's Golf and Country Club is captured nowhere better than from the 18th tee. You're catching your breath, having played a jaw-dropping, 486-yard, dogleg par 4, and you're facing the second blow of one of the most memorable finishing one-two punches in the world. The fabled country club and its highly touted championship course, designed in 1929 by none other than Stanley Thompson, initially served the traveling guests of the Canadian Pacific Railway's Royal York Hotel in Toronto and was originally known as The Royal York Golf Club. Today the clubhouse interior is beautifully refurbished to include top-notch curling facilities and a variety of wonderful dining options where members and guests are treated to an excellent club experience.

St. George's enjoys a storied past like few other clubs in Canada. It has been the host of five Canadian Opens and five LPGA Tour events, as well as numerous national and provincial championships. In 2012, *Golf Digest* ranked the course number 10 in the world outside the United States and first in Canada—its highest international ranking to date.

The 18th, which was lengthened for the 2010 RBC Canadian Open, is a formidable closing hole. A long and accurate tee shot is required to navigate onto the slowly rising and rumpled fairway between bunkers on both the left and right. Confidence in your club selection is crucial on the approach to the green, which is again guarded by treacherous right and left bunkers. Stick it close, and if you can't do that, leave your ball below the hole for a chance at birdie.

Photograph © Clive Barber

ST. THOMAS
Golf & Country Club

3 HOLE

PAR 4 ◆ 413 YARDS

Union, ON
519.631.4800
www.stthomasgolf.com

A sense of the game's and the club's history is with every player, every step of the round at St. Thomas Golf & Country Club. The first nine holes opened in 1899, and ever since the club has grown, adapted, and evolved into a modern-day treasure. A masterful stroke occurred in 1922 when the club, having already relocated twice, hired the incomparable Stanley Thompson to design a new course. The first Thompson nine opened a year later, and when the 18-hole course was completed in 1927, St. Thomas' place in Canadian golf was secured. Legends like Moe Norman, George Knudson, and Mike Weir have won tournaments on this superb test.

As the game changed, Thompson disciple C.E. "Robbie" Robinson added length and five new holes in the 1970s. Between 1995 and 2005, renowned architect Doug Carrick, who honed his craft working with Robinson, created a new master plan. Carrick and restoration specialist Ian Andrew restored the shot values and timeless characteristics of the original Thompson design. Since 2005, Andrew has been the

club's architect. The players of today and tomorrow are the beneficiaries of this masterful lineage.

St. Thomas now plays to 6,779 yards and a par of 72, through the nicely wooded park land setting with valleys and hills, and regular encounters with the meandering Beaver Creek. The 3rd is a wonderful par 4 that is the course's number-one handicap hole. With four tee boxes, it can play as long as 413 yards or as short as 327. However, with Thompson and Robinson, length is never the primary design element. Tee shots must first carry Beaver Creek and find the narrow fairway bordered by the creek on the left and woods on the right. Approach shots must carry the creek again—a mere 15 yards in front of the green—to a putting surface severely sloped back to front. Golfers beware: masters at work.

Photograph by Mark Girdavskas

VESPRA HILLS
Golf Club

PAR 4 ◆ 416 YARDS

Springwater Township, ON
705.721.5831
www.vesprahillsgolfclub.com

Membership certainly has its advantages at Vespra Hills Golf Club. Not only can members choose which two of three nines to play to make up their 18-hole round, they can also reserve times to play the three sister courses at the 54-hole Spring Lakes Golf Club in Stouffville. Even with all the options, it is never long before members include the Homestead nine, with its six challenging and interesting par 4s, two par 3s, and one par 5 on the 3,216-yard, par-35 layout. The nine was built by G. Mac Frost, mostly on what once was his wife Beth's family homestead, hence the name. Homestead winds through mature trees before it makes its way onto the original grain fields and becomes more of a links-style course. The fairways are generous, but the fescue and almost 40-foot elevation change between the 4th and 8th holes add to the Homestead's unique charm and challenges.

The benches at Vespra Hills are made from trees felled on the property, and hole yardage signs are carved into large boulders unearthed during course construction.

At the 3rd hole on Homestead, the boulder reads: par 4, 416 yards. There are four tee decks throughout the course, and the 3rd also plays to 390, 369, and 351 yards. Deceptively difficult, it is risk/reward from the tee, with the conservative route a shot down to the left of the 150-yard marker. Risk-takers try to fly the trees and mounds on the corner, where imperfect attempts can find the creek or its bushy banks. No second shot is easy, as the creek cuts across the fairway while mounds and a large bunker on each side guard the undulating green. Whatever the strategy, daring and prudent players alike are rewarded with a view of a beautiful green complex.

Photographs courtesy of Vespra Hills Golf Club

BAXTER CREEK
Golf Club

PAR 3 ◆ 197 YARDS

Fraserville, ON
705.932.8888
www.baxtercreekgolf.com

Award-winning course architect David L. Moote created in Baxter Creek Golf Club a design approach reminiscent of the celebrated Stanley Thompson/Donald Ross methods that incorporate vintage ambience with the surrounding countryside. Located near the city of Peterborough, this beautifully sculptured course features fairways, greens, and bunkers that replicate many of the appearances of Highland and Carolina golf.

Reminiscent of the par 3 of the world-famous Valhalla Golf Club in Louisville, Kentucky, the 197-yard 8th is a great test of shotmaking skills. The hole is visually a classic with a shallow, kidney-shaped green. A thicket of coniferous trees runs down the left side, and on the right, backing the green, thick fescue and a sentry of 14 juniper pines provide ample protection to this small putting surface. From the elevated tee box and the highest point on the course, a golfer has the visual confidence that par or better is certainly a possibility, but this hole lays in wait for the over-confident shotmaker.

With the ever-changing winds and a challenging distance from all tee boxes, correct club selection is a must. An under-clubbed shot is sure to find one of the three well-positioned sand traps that guard this undulating green short, front, and left. With such a small target, many balls hitting the putting surface will not hold the green and golfers will find themselves frustrated and scrambling to make par on what at first seemed like such a playable hole.

Photograph by RC Media

BEACH GROVE
Golf & Country Club

12 HOLE

PAR 3 ◆ 208 YARDS

Tecumseh, ON
519.979.8090
www.beachgrove.net

Beach Grove Golf & Country Club enthusiastically lives up to its name, with the country club aspect as vitally important to the family-oriented membership as the golf. On an expansive setting on the edges of Lake St. Clair, the club is truly a social focal point with a large boat moorage, oversized outdoor pool, curling rink, high-rise patio deck, lounges, and fine and casual dining all part of the congenial atmosphere. The golf is of the same high standard. Created in the Roaring '20s by legendary architect Stanley Thompson and punctuated by his signature bunkers with their movement and fingers, Beach Grove is a classic park land design with some of the best—and smallest—greens in the province. An enjoyable walk, the course is simultaneously welcoming and challenging.

That variety is evident in the multiple options on the beautiful 12th hole. Depending on which of the five tee decks players chose, this par 3 can play from 156 yards back to 208 yards. And, as importantly, it can play over no water, a bit of water, or over the massive pond along the right side of the hole. From the back tee deck and two others, the pond is simply a reminder to aim for the left side of the small, well-protected green. From the two other tee decks positioned behind the pond—one up on a large mound—the tee shot is entirely over water. The green is guarded by a bunker near the pond's edge on the right, a larger bunker along the left side, and a smaller one behind the green. Sloped back to front to accept tee shots, the putting surface sides are also raised, creating a slight bowl effect that feeds shots into the center—a small assist appreciated by most players.

Photographs by Glenn Gervais

BEACON HALL
Golf Club

PAR 3 ◆ 191 YARDS

Aurora, ON
905.841.9122
www.beaconhall.com

Since its opening on July 1st, 1988, Beacon Hall Golf Club has consistently been ranked among the top 10 courses in Canada. As one of the first equity or member-owned clubs in the country, it remains a golfer's paradise. Director of golf Phil Hardy, who has been with the club since its inception, confirms that Beacon Hall's founders' original vision of this private, gated golf community, just 30 minutes north of Toronto, remains true. The membership is capped at 260 equity members, allowing for "walk on" accessibility to the first tee without reserved tee times, and rounds are routinely played in less than four hours.

After playing back-to-back par 4s through magnificent Carolina pines that cast haunting shadows early in the morning or late in the day, it's a short walk to a spectacular 191-yard, downhill par 3. With whispery pines bordering three sides and feathery fescue in the foreground, there is a sense that the course is building in difficulty with each shot, but this is actually the most sedate of the five par 3s on the course.

Unlike the second green, this putting surface lies on an angle to the center line of the hole. The shot required is a fade. The left side is open with a false front that will repel a shot that falls short of the mark back down to the fairway below. The right pin area is guarded by a five-foot-deep bunker and on the back by several sand and grass bunkers. Fading the ball gives the player almost twice the distance to stop the ball. If you're not fully warmed up by this point you're probably in trouble, because beginning with the 4th Beacon Hall takes it up a notch for a breathtaking journey through rolling forest until you make the turn at the 10th.

Photograph courtesy of Beacon Hall Golf Club

BRAMPTON
Golf Club

16 HOLE

PAR 3 ◆ 212 YARDS

Brampton, ON
905.457.4443
www.bramptongolf.com

The ancient game arrived in the Brampton area, just west of Toronto, in the 1890s, brought along by Irish and Scottish immigrants. They played in the rough fields that are now part of the modern city. Members joined the first club for the princely annual fee of one dollar. Brampton Golf Club was formed in 1921 because, as the local newspaper reported: "Golf is a great game from start to finish, requiring strong nerve, endurance, power of concentration, strength, and sound judgment." Canadian golf legend Stanley Thompson designed the original nine-hole course, and Brampton moved to its present 193-acre site in 1963. On the terrain ideally suited for golf, Thompson protégé C.E. "Robbie" Robinson created the classic layout that has played host to some of Canada's most prestigious tournaments.

Golfers get a sense of Brampton's rich history and links to golf's origins right on the scorecard. In clear lettering, players are encouraged to complete their rounds in four hours and 15 minutes or less, and a "time par" is indicated for each hole.

At the terrific 16th hole, the par is 3 and the par time for the group to finish the hole is three hours and 46 minutes after its start time. To achieve both goals, players face a tee shot of 212 yards from the gold tees and 161 yards from the yellow—the shortest of the five tee boxes—over the Etobicoke Creek to the green 60 feet below. The creek guards the right side of the green, along with a 40-yard-long bunker. There are also bunkers protecting the front left and the back. Club selection is challenging, as the green is 30 yards deep and 25 yards wide. Subtle nuances on the putting surface complete Robinson's deft design.

Photograph courtesy of Brampton Golf Club

CARLETON
Golf & Yacht Club

PAR 3 ◆ 203 YARDS

Manotick, ON
613.692.3531
www.carletongolf.com

Over the first 50 years of Carleton Golf & Yacht Club's dynamic history, it has had the unique distinction of having foursomes representing four generations walking its fairways together. Great-grandparents playing golf with their children, their children's children, and their children is the essence of the club. Carleton has always been and will always be about family. With residences nearby and a course that is not overly long or hilly, Carleton is ideal for players of all generations to enjoy a walk unspoiled.

The pure golf challenges are here too, attested by 1996 and 1997 club champion Brad Fritsch. His family lives on the course that he grew up on, honing his game for the PGA Tour. And the membership includes some of the highest-ranked women players in the region. Carleton's "postage stamp" greens—consistently ranked among the Capital Region's finest—their subtle movement, and the narrow fairways are major factors in the club's legacy of fine players.

The 6th hole is a tough-as-nails par 3 that plays to 203 yards from the back tee, 161 yards from the forward tee. The green initially appears inviting since it's open in the front, but that opening is quite small and framed by bunkers on either side. The putting surface is angled from left to right, which requires a fade with a long iron, a difficult shot with the prevailing wind. When the pin is in the front portion of the green, the subtly designed hole plays a club less than the scorecard distance indicates. It's a good thing to remember, as any shots that go long end up in the thick, penal rough.

Photograph by Scott MacLeod, www.FlagstickGolfPhotography.com

CHERRY HILL
Club

Located in the fertile Niagara Peninsula southwest of Toronto and a short distance from the world-famous Niagara Falls and Buffalo, New York, this historic, private club was founded in 1922. Cherry Hill Club played host in 1972 to the Canadian Open, which was won by Gay Brewer and featured many of the leading names of the game at that time, including Arnold Palmer, Sam Snead, and Gary Player.

Originally designed by renowned golf architect Walter J. Travis, it has recently been artistically re-crafted by Ian Andrew of Ian Andrew Design to maintain the traditions of the course but reflect the new golf club technology.

The 9th hole is a wonderful expression of the beautiful natural setting of Cherry Hill. Though inviting by nature, the odds are not in favor for many golfers on this long par 3, as this uphill hole, with the ever-prevailing southwest winds, requires focus and correct club selection. The view from the tee box to green appears straightforward and a player, if he is the right vintage, can relive the dramatic hole-in-one that professional Raymond Floyd made at the 1982 Canadian PGA Championship. This inviting green is well protected by deep bunkers left and right, and the recent removal of many of the trees surrounding the green now creates a constant air flow that can easily affect the shape of a shot onto the green. Backing the bunker, a stand of trees ensures that any shot straying to the right will land in a world of trouble.

Photographs by John Gall

COBBLE BEACH
Golf Links

PAR 3 ◆ 171 YARDS

Owen Sound, ON
888.278.8112
www.cobblebeach.com

Award-winning Canadian architect Doug Carrick has created magnificent courses around the world, including some legendary seaside links reminiscent of a classic Scottish design. In creating Cobble Beach Golf Links, Carrick brings all of his experience and mastery of terrain to the waterfront plateau overlooking Georgian Bay. Starting at the gracious Nantucket-style clubhouse, the course winds through open meadows bordered by dense forests, revealing stunning views of the Bay and the spectacular four-season community. The 8th, 9th, and 18th holes are sculpted along the edge of the shoreline, adding to the drama of play. When it opened in 2007, Cobble Beach was named one of the top 10 best new courses in the world and the best new course in Ontario.

Paying homage to the original home of golf, Carrick fashioned run-and-tumble fairways and pot bunkers, offering players options at every turn. That creativity and enjoyment is available to all, as the course plays from 5, 157 yards from the forward tees up to a maximum of 7,174 yards for the big hitters.

Commanding a panoramic view of one of the most scenic areas in the province, the 17th hole is aptly named Lighthouse for its distinctive structure silhouetted against the glistening waters of Georgian Bay. Playing from 107 yards back to 171 yards, this inspiring par 3 plays downhill to a spacious green that appears to fall off into the Bay. The marsh along the right side expands into a pond just before the green and circles around behind the multi-leveled putting surface. Three deep bunkers guard the right front of the green. A pot bunker and greenside bunker protect the left. It's a devil of a green to hit, yet this classic mid-length par 3 nestled in an idyllic setting at Cobble Beach is certainly not one to be missed.

Photograph © Clive Barber

CREDIT VALLEY
Golf and Country Club

PAR 3 ◆ 201 YARDS

Mississauga, ON
905.275.2505
www.creditvalleygolf.com

Legendary Canadian golfing icon Al Balding—Credit Valley Golf and Country Club's first golf professional and honorary member until his passing in 2006—suggested that the 11th at Credit Valley is one of the best par 3s he has ever played. As the first Canadian winner of a PGA Tour event on American soil, he could certainly speak from broad experience and was emphatic not just about the playability, but also the grandeur of the hole. His passion for the 11th is experienced by golfers of every level, as this majestic hole captures much of the essence of the course as a whole.

From the five sets of tees, shots must carry the Credit River, which cuts diagonally across the length of the hole. The aim should be for a soft landing on a very narrow and long green. A mishit shot or misjudgment of the strength of the constantly swirling winds, influenced by the valley wall and a bank of mature trees behind the green, results in many a ball being captured by the river or the three strategically placed bunkers. The combination of river and trees will challenge any player's focus.

This green slopes from left to right and back to front, so if your ball does find one of the hazards or ends up left of the green you are left with an extremely difficult up and down. A ball landing softly short and to the right of the pin, regardless of the pin's location on the green, will provide a good opportunity for par or better. Number 11 definitely proves that accuracy takes priority over length.

Photograph by Mike Bell, Photoscape Photography

CROSSWINDS
Golf & Country Club

PAR 3 ◆ 178 YARDS

Burlington, ON
905.319.5991
www.crosswindsgolf.com

Crosswinds Golf & Country Club has twice been ranked as a top 10 best bang for your buck course by *Ontario Golf Magazine*, and this 18-hole championship layout continues to provide challenge and enjoyment for all skill levels at a reasonable price. Located a short distance from Hamilton and Toronto, the course features wide fairways, plenty of sand, strategically placed water hazards on 11 holes, and undulating greens that run true throughout the golfing season.

Crosswinds' signature 5th hole embodies the essence of the course's personality: constant wind, a green that is comparatively small, and a water hazard that encircles the green like a horseshoe. Luck is definitely required, as three of the four sets of tee boxes must carry this liquid distraction to safely reach the putting surface and to avoid the four bunkers that also stand guard front and back.

While hitting what might seem like the perfect shot, watch out for the large rocks that protect the green and deflect balls into one of the hazards. Once safely on the green the contour is right-to-left, and if you judge your speed incorrectly a three-putt can be a real possibility. Par or better and you will have bragging rights in the clubhouse following your round.

Photograph by Chris Gallow

ELMIRA
Golf Club

PAR 3 ◆ 193 YARDS

Elmira, ON
519.669.1652
www.elmiragolfclub.com

Meandering through the rolling terrain of the Eldale Valley, with lush trees providing seclusion along fairways and around greens and Larches Creek adding charm and challenge to 12 of the 18 holes, Elmira Golf Club is a shotmaker's delight, yet still welcoming to higher handicap and even beginning players. The five sets of tees allow all players to enjoy as much of a challenge as they choose. The yellow tees set the course at less than 5,000 yards, an ideal introduction to this well-maintained layout and the game itself. At par 70, the black tees offer a more than 6,300-yard test that—with just two par 5s—places the emphasis on club selection, accuracy, and course management. The enticing 11th hole is a perfect example.

The tall trees along both sides and behind the green not only provide beautiful natural definition to this well-designed par 3, but also help focus players' attention on a deceptively difficult tee shot. The trees often offer conflicting signals too, as the wind can swirl on this part of the course and make proper club and target selection critical.

The red tees require a shot of 110 yards to the center of the large green. However, from the black tees at 193 yards and the blue tees at 169 yards, the putting surface looks much smaller. A large bunker protects the left side of the elevated green, the bank on the right drops off sharply, and the series of mounds behind the wide but relatively shallow green present difficult recovery shots. Even when tee shots reach the green, the subtle undulations and the trees' shadows make par a good score at the 11th.

Photograph courtesy of Elmira Golf Club

ESSEX
Golf & Country Club

17 HOLE

PAR 3 ◆ 219 YARDS

Windsor, ON
519.734.7816
www.essexgolf.com

The name Donald Ross is spoken with reverence by golfers the world over for the master architect's unique ability to create courses that challenge and inspire players generation after generation. A perfect example of Ross's timeless genius is Essex Golf & Country Club. Players walking the immaculate, tree-lined course today can only marvel that Essex was created back in 1929 with horses pulling ploughs. Yet despite the advances in construction and golf club technology, the par-71, 6,703-yard masterpiece is still as demanding and enjoyable as the day it opened. In eloquent testimony to the Ross design, Essex hosted the 1976 PGA Tour Canadian Open, the 1998 LPGA Tour Canadian Championship, and the 2002 Champions Tour Senior Open. For men and women, juniors and seniors, professional and recreational players, Ross' Essex layout is as welcoming as the club's red brick, Tudor-style clubhouse.

At the par-3 17th hole, the master's skills are on full display. Ross is known for his large, undulating, and sculptured greens. The target is three-tiered—219 yards from the back tee, 132 yards from the most forward of the four tee boxes. The putting surface slopes dramatically back to front, with a ridge running diagonally left to right. As Ross intended, no putt on this green is easy, as each one is uphill, downhill, or sidehill. The only straight putts are tap ins.

Five bunkers and a series of mounds guard the 17th, and any shot past the green requires clever negotiation of the tiers. Many players play it short, hoping to chip it close for a par. Down through the ages, Ross offers golfers this examination of their game with par being excellent, bogey average, and higher scores still not uncommon.

Photograph by Joan Lam

GRANITE
Golf Club

HOLE 4

PAR 3 ◆ 176 YARDS

Stouffville, ON
905.642.4416
www.granitegolfclub.ca

Designed by the internationally renowned Canadian golf course architect Thomas McBroom, the award-winning Granite Golf Club is recognized as Canada's premier private family golf club. Opened in 2000, the club encouraged more family play and became the first in Canada to establish the CJGA Family Tee Program. Its continued dedication to youth led to the club being selected as the home and Provincial training center for Team Ontario's junior golf athletes.

As you stand on the elevated tee box, the first par 3 on the course has intimidation written all over it. Unlike most par 3s, where the golfer would focus on the pin position and the contours of the green to ensure proper club selection and ball placement, on hole 4 a golfer's first view is of the numerous perils awaiting any errant shot. Wetlands extending from tee to green require a high, lofted shot to land softly on this small, oval-shaped green. Shots that play over the hazard but land short of the putting surface require a steep uphill lob shot and must be hit with confidence, as the green runs back to front and any ball hit too softly will end up with the player repeating a similar shot, this time to save par.

Players who over-club will face a sentinel of deciduous trees a few paces off the back of this oval green, and will find themselves above the pin with a torturous pitch now required to land softly on the green. Large swales in the center of the green will often boost the speed of the ball, and a golfer can find himself back in front of the green in long, lush grass requiring another perfect lob shot and another attempt to stay on the putting surface.

Photograph © Clive Barber

HURON OAKS
Golf Club

PAR 3 ◆ 178 YARDS

Bright's Grove, ON
519.869.4231
www.huronoaks.com

Huron Oaks Golf Club, in a beautiful park land setting on the shores of Lake Huron, has a long and colorful history. Golf fans recognize Bright's Grove as the hometown of Canadian golf legend and 2003 Masters Champion Mike Weir. However, not all are aware that the PGA Tour star virtually grew up and learned the game at Huron Oaks. In the early 1900s, it was a six-hole layout on the grounds of beer baron John Labatt's summer residence. New owners expanded it to nine holes in 1938, and the Labatt Victorian mansion became the clubhouse. In the 1950s, the back nine was added, and some 20 years later the holes nearest the lake expanded into what is now the 6,518-yard, par-72 course. Charming and fit for a grand scenic stroll, historic Huron Oaks now includes a residential development and new pro shop. John Labatt probably wouldn't recognize his old holiday retreat today, but like the current members and public players, he would hopefully wholeheartedly approve.

The 15th is a beautiful hole that is expertly designed to challenge players from all three tee boxes. The large pond dominates this par-3 hole and players on the 178-yard blue championship tees and 142-yard white tees must carry its entire length. From the 119-yard yellow tees, it is possible to skim the corner of the water, but this requires avoiding the well-placed bunkers in front, on the right, and behind the green. The large kidney-shaped putting surface is undulating, slopes back to front, and runs smooth and fast. And to top it all off, the 15th usually plays into the wind, making it as challenging as it is beautiful.

Photograph by Trevor Taylor

ISLINGTON
Golf Club

PAR 3 ◆ 144 YARDS

Islington, ON
416.231.1114
www.islingtongolfclub.com

While Islington Golf Club was first conceived in 1913, WWI delayed its evolution for a decade. In 1923, famed Canadian course architect Stanley Thompson was retained at a fee of $25,000 to lay out and supervise construction of the course by a crew of 50 men and 20 teams of horses. Although there have been minor changes to the hole sequence over the years, the course still plays close to its original design and remains a treasure in Canadian golf. It stands as a testament to Thompson's brilliance at creating great golf in natural settings by drawing up individual course characters at each site.

Thompson creates drama off the tee on the 6th hole—the shortest of the four par 3s—on a tight park land layout that plays a very challenging 6,472 yards, par 72 from the tips. The prevailing wind can wreak havoc with the ball on this tricky 144-yard hole, where golfers can hit anything from a wedge to a 7-iron depending on the pin position and the wind. You don't want to make an error in club selection or you'll be in big trouble, and there have been a lot of errors made on this hole.

That trouble starts with four dramatic bunkers carved into the sides of the elevated green that encircles the tight landing area, leaving little room for error. Then there's the three-tiered green that can quickly discourage a timid putter or confound a pro. It's a spectacular hole, even if you're unlucky enough to score a bogey.

Photograph © Clive Barber

KAWARTHA
Golf & Country Club

PAR 3 ◆ 151 YARDS

Peterborough, ON
705.743.3737
www.kawarthagolf.ca

This challenging 18-hole course, designed by renowned architect Stanley Thompson, is located in one of Ontario's most beautiful regions, just 45 minutes northeast of Toronto in the Kawartha Lakes area. Founded over 80 years ago, ranked the 24th best classic course in Canada by *Golfweek Magazine,* and recognized year after year as one of the top 25 courses in the province, Kawartha Golf & Country Club provides impeccable course conditions, mature trees reflecting the beauty of the region, and natural tranquility. Families and friends gather at the club to enjoy golf, social activities, and great food.

Renowned for its par 3s, Kawartha boasts some of the most challenging in the province. The 8th hole upholds the finest traditions of the game, as it rewards precision and stands out as a high point on a course in which every hole is a memorable challenge. Nestled between two deep bunkers, play your tee shot off line to either side and par is just a dream.

The entrance to Kawartha is one of the most impressive drives you will ever experience. The deciduous trees that line the quarter-mile driveway are a brilliant green in the summer months and an orchestra of oranges, bronzes, and reds as the cooler fall weather approaches, creating a Canadian experience equivalent to Magnolia Lane at Augusta National. This in itself will be a highlight of your day.

Karwartha Golf & Country Club is the proud, long-standing host of the Kawartha Men's Invitational, a three-day tournament that attracts amateur golfers from across Canada and the United States. The tournament began in 1946 and continues to draw a full field of players and spectators, which has included well-known golfers such as Ben Kern, Moe Norman, and PGA Tour Player Jon Mills. Today it is one of the only three-day invitationals in Ontario.

Photograph courtesy of Kawartha Golf & Country Club

KING'S FOREST
Golf Club

PAR 3 ◆ 248 YARDS

Hamilton, ON
905.546.4781
www.golfhamilton.ca

Resting at the foot of the Niagara Escarpment and in the heart of the picturesque Red Hill Valley, King's Forest Golf Club is recognized as one of Ontario's premier public courses. Completed in 1973 and managed by the City of Hamilton, this rolling layout features outstanding elevated tee shots, challenging doglegs, and six holes with Red Hill Creek running through. This beautiful and challenging course has been host to prestigious events such as as the Ontario Men's Amateur and Canadian University Championships, further cementing its status as one of the most highly regarded golf facilities in Canada.

A long, downhill par 3 is considered by many as the most challenging and exhilarating hole to play on any golf course, as a golfer's ability to judge distance, anticipate wind direction, and manage club selection are strategic—any miscalculation and opportunities for par quickly diminish. The 5th at King's Forest is a fine example of a daring golf hole, the longest par 3 on the course; it lures players in with a false sense of ease. There are no visible bunkers, minimal trees, and the contours of the green funnel balls toward the putting surface if hit just right or left of the surface.

With the hole nestled 100 feet below and the Niagara Escarpment as its backdrop, the primary needs are judging the direction of the wind and selecting the appropriate club. The green is sheltered and the flag will often be still. Any ball hit long on this hole will find a deep drop-off and a difficult uphill wedge second shot. A ball that falls short on this green will prove to be an intricate up and down.

Photograph courtesy of City of Hamilton, King's Forest Golf Club

LADIES' GOLF CLUB
of Toronto

PAR 3 ◆ 179 YARDS

Thornhill, ON
905.889.3531
www.ladiesgolfclub.com

Ada Mackenzie was not only a superb golfer—she won 10 national amateur championships and was Canada's female athlete of the year in 1933—she was also a visionary. To fulfill her dream of a golf club where women could play without restriction, and after much hard work and fundraising, Mackenzie and colleagues purchased a 130-acre farm a few miles north of the nation's largest city. The finest woman golfer of the day commissioned the nation's best architect of any era, Stanley Thompson. In 1924, Ladies' Golf Club of Toronto was established; it's still the only golf club in North America owned and operated by women. Nine holes debuted in 1925, with the full 18-hole course opening the following year.

Ideal for women players yet a challenge for the best male golfers, it plays to just over 6,000 yards from the longest of the four sets of tees. Three additional holes were added in 1963 so that members and guests could play rounds of nine or 18 holes before enjoying the many amenities of the stately clubhouse.

A fine example of Thompson's masterful design is the par-3 16th hole. Whether playing from the red tee at 108 yards or back at the blue tee at 179 yards, golfers have Thompson's visual aid: the "V" formed by the trees behind the green aligns with the left center of the putting surface, the ideal aiming point. It serves as a good reference, as players must avoid the creek crossing the fairway—134 yards from the blue tee—and the bunkers guarding both sides of a green that slopes back to front and right to left. The 16th is a gem of a hole on a classic Thompson course.

Photograph courtesy of Ladies' Golf Club of Toronto

LOCH MARCH

Golf & Country Club

Kanata, ON
613.839.5885
www.lochmarch.com

Named for the surrounding March Highlands, the "Loch" in Loch March Golf & Country Club is a nod to the owner's Scottish heritage and the property's lake. Since the 1987 opening, guests at Loch March have experienced a traditional sense of arrival. The hostesses greet players as the shuttle brings them to and from the parking lot. The 10,000-square-foot, Tudor-style clubhouse, with its expansive lounge, indoor and outdoor restaurants, banquet room with wraparound balcony, and 5,000-square-foot terrace, sprawls at the top of the driveway. Offering every amenity, the clubhouse overlooks the course and the 44,000-square-foot putting green, the practice range with bentgrass target greens, and a 100-yard bentgrass tee deck. At the "exclusively public" Loch March, attention to countless details adds up to a memorable golf experience.

When Loch March owner and architect Mark Fuller walked his dramatic Canadian Shield property designing his course, he saw an opportunity to utilize water flow and create ponds. Instead of making the now cliché island green, however, Fuller and designer Gordon Witteveen created an island tee. The 16th at Loch March is a unique par 3 that dramatically engages players at every tee box. At 197 yards from the back tees, golfers play over the island and lake; from the four other tees, they play from the island over the water. The tee design is inspired and the green complex challenging, with the large, elevated putting surface having three distinct tiers. The three bunkers starting well in front of the green, the massive bunker on the right that reaches from the front to the far right-middle of the green, and the mounding and trees surrounding enhance the optical and very real challenge of the 16th. With Fuller's inspiration and under superintendent Witteveen's care, Geoffrey Cornish would be well pleased.

Photograph by Michelle Valberg

197

LONDON HUNT
and Country Club

PAR 3 ◆ 216 YARDS

London, ON
519.471.6430
www.londonhuntclub.com

On 275 acres of beautifully wooded and rolling Southern Ontario terrain sits 1885-established London Hunt and Country Club, one of North America's oldest and most prestigious clubs. Unique for its *entente cordiale* of fox hunting, tennis, skeet, and trapshooting, London Hunt is also home to one of master architect Robert Trent Jones' finest golf courses. The first nine holes opened in 1904, with the course expanding to 18 holes 13 years later. In 1960, a year after the Jones course was completed, London Hunt moved to its present and permanent location. Testament to the quality of the design, London Hunt has hosted numerous elite events including the 1970 Canadian Open, the 2006 Canadian Women's Open, and the 2010 Canadian Amateur.

The 2nd hole is a classic Jones par 3. It plays over water from the championship tees at 216 yards, with four other tees varying the length down to 109 yards. Three elegantly mounded bunkers guard the green, two on the right and one on the left. The hole is slightly downhill with the prevailing wind from the right, the large stones of the wall buttressing the front of the green clearly defining the water's edge. Typical of Jones' greens, the 2nd is large—averaging 10,000 square feet—with as much as a four-club difference between a front and back pin. When the pin is front left, just over the water and short of the bunker, par is an excellent score.

Photograph by Nicole Osborne, NEO Image Creations

LOOKOUT POINT
Country Club

PAR 3 ◆ 175 YARDS

Fonthill, ON
905.892.2639
www.lopcc.com

It is rare to play golf on a true classic course that awards accuracy over the "let 'er rip" monster courses that are so prevalent in the modern era. Created in 1919 and opened in 1922 by Golf Hall of Fame inductee Walter J. Travis, who believed that "diversity of play should be the aim of a first-class course," Lookout Point Country Club remains a player's experience. Located in the fruit orchard region of the Niagara Peninsula, it is the home course of Canada's most recognized amateur woman golfer, Marlene Stewart-Streit. At just over 6,600 yards, the course is not long by today's standards but it is continually ranked in Canada's top 100 for the challenge, panoramic views, and vintage feel with narrow tree-lined fairways and small sloping greens.

The 8th was at one time the 17th when Lookout Point was a stop on the professional men's golf tour in the 1930s, and one can still envision the likes of Ben Hogan and Byron Nelson as they made the walk, single file up the dirt path, to see if they had an opportunity for birdie on this demanding par 3.

Presbyterian Pass is its moniker, as the hole has always been portrayed as "straight and narrow." When the constant winds are blowing, a Hail Mary approach to hitting onto the putting surface is best, as the green sits 60 feet above the tee box—a difference of one to three clubs in shot selection. The green is the largest on the course, and front and left bunkers provide ample protection for shots that fall short. No matter your score, take a moment to look east and enjoy the vistas of the tee box below and the skyline and mist of Niagara Falls in the distance.

Photographs courtesy of Lookout Point Country Club

LOYALIST
Country Club

PAR 3 ◆ 166 YARDS

Bath, ON
613.352.5152
www.loyalistcc.com

This Ted Baker/Cornish Robinson-designed course features four sets of tee blocks and has, since its opening in 1998, become one of the most popular and challenging golf courses in the historic Kingston region of Ontario. Though not overly long at 6,700 yards, Loyalist Country Club is always in prime condition—it has hosted many major provincial tournaments, including the 2012 Ontario Ladies Championship and a PGA Tour of Canada event in 2014.

With water coming into play on 12 of the holes and deep fescue everywhere, golfers will find this beautiful course a great test of their game. Standing on the tee overlooking the 166-yard, par-3 8th hole, golfers can feel the strength of the prevailing winds off nearby Lake Ontario. A shot hit just left or right of the putting surface will find the downslope and most likely bounce into the fescue. Balls hit too long will certainly find deep grass and an almost impossible up and down to save par.

To add to the challenge of the 8th, the green is protected by two deep pot bunkers and the fine Ohio White sand, requiring a masterful bunker shot to land softly on this long, narrow, undulating putting surface. Avoid having a downhill putt, as this hole features one of the fastest bentgrass greens on the course. A par here and you will have played the hole better than most.

Photographs by Scott MacLeod, www.FlagstickGolfPhotography.com

MEADOWBROOK
Golf & Country Club

PAR 3 ◆ 200 YARDS

Gormley, ON
905.887.5801
www.meadowbrookgolf.net

The pristine rolling fairways, towering trees, smooth bunkers, and manicured greens of Meadowbrook Golf & Country Club belie the pioneer efforts of its founding members. It was their physical labor, time, and donated resources that formed the club in 1962. That devotion and close fellowship forged the character of the club that endures today. Over the years, Meadowbrook has evolved and matured into one of the best courses in the province, having hosted the Ontario PGA Championship and the Canadian Tournament Players Championship. In the early 2000s, one of Canada's finest golf architects, Graham Cooke, reconstructed two holes, lengthened six holes, created new tee boxes on four holes, and redesigned the practice green and range. Continuing improvements have culminated in a championship course playing from 5,300 yards to almost 7,000 yards that is a challenge and pleasure from all tee boxes.

Since its founding, Meadowbrook has been a player's course. The par-3 12th hole is a fine example of the tests the course presents. Welcoming all players, it ranges from 90 yards off the forward tees to a stout 200 from the tips. The water is a factor from every tee, especially with a prevailing wind visiting from the golfer's right. Two bunkers outline the back and left portions of the green, with the back bunker presenting a challenging second shot to a surface sloping toward the water. Any bailouts to the right and long find mounding above the surface of the green, with thick rough providing challenges for the best short game. Tough par 3, two-mounded green; just as the Meadowbrook founders would play it.

Photographs by Jim Speirs

MILL RUN
Golf Club

PAR 3 • 194 YARDS

Uxbridge, ON
800.465.8633
www.golfmillrun.com

The beautiful rolling hills surrounding Uxbridge, just 25 miles northeast of Toronto, provide an ideal setting for golf. In 1986, Mill Run Golf Club debuted 18 spectacular holes, two nines that are now known as The Grist and The Wheel. The Grist is truly a walker's delight and offers a combination of signature holes and natural beauty. The Wheel, also ideal for golfers who enjoy a good walk unspoiled, provides a demanding test with several holes calling for negotiation of water hazards and tree-narrowed fairways. By 2007, Mill Run was firmly established as one of Southern Ontario's finest facilities when the third nine, The Grind, was completed to meet the growing demands of golfers in the Durham Region and Greater Toronto Area. Providing Mill Run with 27 holes of championship golf, The Grind takes advantage of some of the most dramatic terrain in the area. The breathtaking scenery, elevation changes, and well-designed holes combine to make a memorable golf experience.

Set back in the tall pines and defined by flowing golden fescue, the par-3 7th hole on The Grind has a Carolina feel to it. The tee shot from the four tee boxes, ranging from 110 yards to 194 yards, requires careful club selection. A valley and greenside bunker demand a forced carry the entire distance to the green. The putting surface slopes significantly from left to right, so even when the pin is positioned on the right portion of the green the target must be the left side. Getting there is just half the fun. The challenge of the 7th green is a combination of the slope, subtle contours, and meticulous maintenance that ensures putts roll true—and quickly.

Photograph by Stuart Brindle

OAK BAY
Golf & Country Club

15 HOLE

PAR 3 ◆ 170 YARDS

Port Severn, ON
705.538.0893
www.oakbaygolf.com

On the eastern shores of Georgian Bay in the heart of southern Muskoka, one of North America's most sought-after vacation areas, is one of Ontario's finest new golf courses. The spectacular Oak Bay Golf & Country Club, designed by respected Canadian golf architect Shawn Watters, is the hub of a master-planned residential community that is the essence of cottage country lifestyle blended with casual elegance. Complete with a golf clubhouse and fitness center, marina, nature trails, and a swimming pool, the Oak Bay property offers a relaxed and enjoyable lifestyle experience. Set in the rugged Ontario woodlands and featuring dramatic rock outcroppings, subtle elevation changes, exhilarating carries over wetlands, and captivating views of Georgian Bay, the golf course reveals the terrain's nuances and timeless natural beauty.

One look from the tee is all it takes to understand why the 15th hole is known as one of Canada's must-play holes. This hole is a classic example of a designer's ability to transform an impasse into a golf hole that all players can enjoy. Spanning a stretch of wetlands between two peninsulas, Oak Bay's 15th hole is a memorable par 3 that is scenic, challenging, and enjoyable from all tee boxes. Whether from the back tee at 170 yards or from the forward tee at 68 yards, the 15th plays across the wetlands into the prevailing wind off the Bay.

Making club selection even more critical, the green is elevated. The combination of an uphill shot and the wind can mean as much as a two-club difference. The putting surface is receptive but undulating, and guarded by bunkers front-left and right, and back right. No matter the score, the 15th at Oak Bay is unforgettable.

Photograph by Amy Lepp

OAK BAY
Golf & Country Club

17 HOLE

PAR 3 ◆ 200 YARDS

Port Severn, ON
705.538.0893
www.oakbaygolf.com

Though just a 90-minute drive north of Toronto, Oak Bay Golf & Country Club seems worlds away from urban sprawl. The beautiful shoreline of Georgian Bay along the expansive Oak Bay property is one of the largest freshwater archipelagos in the world, home to hundreds of plants, mammals, birds, and fish, including designated rare species. Indeed, in 2004 the United Nations Educational, Scientific, and Cultural Organization (UNESCO) designated the Eastern Georgian Bay coast as a World Biosphere Reserve. From the outset, the master-planned community of Oak Bay was designed and built with its unique location and sensitive surrounding habitats in mind. As a testament to this, 95 acres of the project has been given over to the Georgian Bay Land Trust to be held in perpetuity to ensure its preservation.

The remarkable natural setting is evident throughout this spectacular golf course, and nowhere more dramatically than on the 17th hole. With a stunning view from all four tee boxes of the rock outcroppings, this par 3 plays to a daunting 200 yards straight over water from the back tees all the way down to 128 yards from the forward tees, set beside the pond. The large green curls out on a point, seemingly to the shore of Georgian Bay, so any shots challenging a back-right pin risk splashing if short, long, or too far right. A series of bunkers guard the left side of the large putting surface, leading to second shots with clear views of the Bay, its shoreline, islands, and cottages. A par on this pristine hole will go a long way toward preserving the round.

Photograph by Amy Lepp

PORT CARLING
Golf & Country Club

16 HOLE

PAR 3 ◆ 188 YARDS

Port Carling, ON
705.765.6600
www.portcarlinggc.com

One of Ontario's true golf masterpieces is Port Carling Golf & Country Club, located in the beautiful Lake District of Muskoka, a few hours north of Toronto. This 18-hole, 6,400-yard par 70 has been the recipient of industry and media kudos for its overall playing experience since its opening in 1991.

In 2007, international golf architects Thomas McBroom and Associates redesigned the course so that it would become not only one of the province's best golf layouts, but one of North America's premier golf properties as well. Through a staged rebuilding program—which included repositioning tee boxes and fairways, replacing all the greens to premium bentgrass, and reshaping the bunkers—McBroom enhanced the natural features of the rugged land into a must-play golfing experience.

This par 3 is a wonderful example of McBroom's ability to incorporate all that nature has to offer. The hole is visually beautiful, yet requires concentration and shotmaking ability to avoid the potential dangers that await an uninformed player. Standing on the tee box, players are aware of the large, three-level green and the deep, white Temiska sand bunkers at the middle back and right front of the green. Be mindful of the wind direction—take note of the trees surrounding the tee box and what direction the flag is blowing, as the ever-changing winds and the pin placement will make a difference of up to two clubs. A ball held up by the wind will find the water, but a calculated shot will find triumph.

Photograph courtesy of Port Carling Golf & Country Club

ST. ANDREW'S
Valley Golf Club

PAR 3 ◆ 224 YARDS

Aurora, ON
905.727.7888
www.standrewsvalley.com

There are golf courses that are challenging and others that are fun to play. In the hands of celebrated architect Rene Muylaert, St. Andrew's Valley Golf Club, located just minutes north of Toronto, is a masterful combination of the two. Spreading out from the stately clubhouse, reminiscent of Augusta National with its large welcoming verandas, the stadium-style layout Muylaert created on the 176 acres of gently rolling countryside offers an enticing blend of lush fairways, sand, and water on almost every hole. With five tee decks, golfers are offered plenty of options: you can play from 5,530 yards back to a robust 7,315 yards, where the rating is 74.8—one of the highest in the province.

The last three of the five par 5s are over 600 yards. With the headwaters of the Holland River nearby, St. Andrew's Valley has water hazards on 14 holes that are spiced with 100 bunkers. One of the most dramatic design features is the infamous waste area on the 6th hole.

Muylaert was encouraged to "think big" while designing the course, and he followed through superbly on this beautiful hole. The 224-yard par 3—one of five on the course—is called Arizona for good reason. On the tees, golfers are presented with the intimidating view of Ontario's largest waste bunker. Inspired by the desert courses of the American Southwest, Arizona's back tee demands a 180-yard carry over sand, gravel, and boulders. Getting over, or through, the area is just the beginning. The massive green has three distinct terraces with severe slopes between them, ensuring that each visit to Arizona is challenging and fun in equal measure.

Photograph by Michael Miller

TURNBERRY
Golf Club

PAR 3 ◆ 156 YARDS

Brampton, ON
905.500.4653
www.turnberrygolf.ca

How often does a golfer have the opportunity to play a course that resembles the fine links-style courses of the British Isles, is close to a major urban center, and can be played in three hours? Welcome to Turnberry Golf Club, Ontario's only Championship short course.

Turnberry is unlike any other golf experience in the Greater Toronto Area, with 16 par 3s and two challenging par 4s reminiscent of the Arran Course, the nine-hole short course in Turnberry, Scotland, where professionals can be seen improving their course management skills. Standing on the 443-yard first tee, a panoramic view spans undulating fairways with golden fescue and white signature sand bunkers. The course is a challenge for the most experienced of putters, especially with Turnberry's exceptional green complexes and severely undulated greens.

The signature 16th hole has an "all or nothing" tee shot, forcing the golfer to reach the green in one or be met with a large water feature. Too much club and a phalanx of fescue waits behind the green; not enough club and you are in the water, greatly minimizing any chance for par. With a green that severely slopes from back to front, any shot past the pin will result in a chip or putt that will be difficult to stop, requiring a well-executed golf shot directed below the pin for any chance at par or better. At this point in the round, according to designer Cam Tyers, players could be called upon to hit an exacting tee shot—or pay the price. If the wind is blowing, you will truly feel the challenge of managing your ball flight while reflecting on what it would be like playing in the British Open.

Photograph © Clive Barber

ST. ANDREW'S
East Golf & Country Club

PAR 3 ◆ 150 YARDS

Stouffville, ON
905.640.4444
www.standrewseast.com

St. Andrew's East Golf & Country Club offers captivating views throughout the 170-acre property just north of Toronto. Formerly a cattle ranch, the lush natural site has been enhanced by the planting of more than 6,400 trees, creating a uniquely verdant and secluded retreat for the St. Andrew's member-owners. The natural beauty and unique isolation of individual holes is on full display at the par-3 4th.

When players arrive at the elevated tee, they immediately know why this classic short hole is named Vista. The four tee boxes—stretching the hole from 118 yards to 150 yards—are approximately 50 feet above the green, providing ideal spots to enjoy the captivating view framed by a kettle lake, marsh, and forest beyond. The wooded backdrop, beautiful in every season, is home to birches, red hawthorns, pines, bull rushes, and other species too numerous to name.

A three-tiered green makes proper club selection vital. The putting surface is kidney-shaped with a large bunker on the left that stretches almost the width of the green, including an island mound of grass residing within. Hidden from view is a small bunker at the back center of the green, with a third bunker at the front right clearly in focus. Last but not least, the slope behind slides severely to the water's edge. There is at least a two-club difference between front and back pin placements. Any wayward shots that carry down the slope beyond the green will find themselves in a watery grave. Perhaps most difficult is concentrating on golf while in Vista's idyllic setting, with its raised elevation, wildlife, and spectacular scenery.

Photographs by David Goldsman

VESPRA HILLS
Golf Club

PAR 3 ◆ 176 YARDS

Springwater Township, ON
705.721.5831
www.vesprahillsgolfclub.com

In the high sandy ridges of Springwater Township just outside the city of Barrie, Vespra Hills Golf Club offers members and their guests three distinct championship nine-hole courses. The first of the nines to open, Sand Hills, meanders through mature trees on the highest ridges of the 270-acre property, providing spectacular views. Sand Hills was designed and built by G. "Mac" Frost, who was inducted into the Ontario Golf Hall of Fame in 2005. Mac was recognized in the golf industry for his innovative thinking and devotion to the development and preservation of the game. A governor of the RCGA, president of the OGA, head of the Greens Superintendents Association, and the first regional head of the National Golf Course Owners Association, Mac said about creating Vespra Hills: "I've learned a fair bit about golf in the last 50 years or so, and I really ought to put it somewhere!"

His vast experience and knowledge of the game are displayed on each of Sand Hills' challenging and delightful holes. The 5th hole demands that golf rarity: a straight tee shot. This beautiful par 3—one of three par 3s on this 3,274-yard, par-35 nine—falls off on the left side of the putting surface, which is protected by two front-right bunkers. Trees line the back and right of the green, where the thick forest valley gathers errant shots. As Mac advised with a smile, anything in the middle will be fine.

Photograph courtesy of Vespra Hills Golf Club

SPECTACULAR GOLF

ONTARIO TEAM
ASSOCIATE PUBLISHER: Marc Zurba
GRAPHIC DESIGNER: Jen Ray
EDITOR : Michael Cunningham
CONTRIBUTING WRITER: Brent Long
CONTRIBUTING WRITER: Hal Quinn
PRODUCTION COORDINATOR: Shellye Thomas

HEADQUARTERS TEAM
PUBLISHER: Brian G. Carabet
PUBLISHER: John A. Shand
SENIOR GRAPHIC DESIGNER: Emily A. Kattan
GRAPHIC DESIGNER: Lauren Schneider
MANAGING EDITOR: Lindsey Wilson
EDITOR: Nick Bridwell
EDITOR: Nicole Pearce
EDITOR: Megan Winkler
MANAGING PRODUCTION COORDINATOR: Kristy Randall
TRAFFIC SUPERVISOR: Drea Williams
ADMINISTRATIVE COORDINATOR: Amanda Mathers
ADMINISTRATIVE ASSISTANT: Aubrey Grunewald

PANACHE PARTNERS, LLC
CORPORATE HEADQUARTERS
1424 Gables Court
Plano, TX 75075
469.246.6060
www.panache.com

Credit Valley Golf and Country Club, page 177

THE PANACHE COLLECTION

Dream Homes Series

An Exclusive Showcase of the Finest Architects, Designers and Builders

Carolinas, Chicago, Coastal California, Colorado, Deserts, Florida, Georgia, Los Angeles, Metro New York, Michigan, Minnesota, New England, New Jersey, Northern California, Ohio & Pennsylvania, Pacific Northwest, Philadelphia, South Florida, Southwest, Tennessee, Texas, Washington, D.C., Extraordinary Homes California

Spectacular Homes Series

An Exclusive Showcase of the Finest Interior Designers

California, Carolinas, Chicago, Colorado, Florida, Georgia, Heartland, London, Michigan, Minnesota, New England, Metro New York, Ohio & Pennsylvania, Pacific Northwest, Philadelphia, South Florida, Southwest, Tennessee, Texas, Toronto, Washington, D.C., Western Canada

Perspectives on Design Series

Design Philosophies Expressed by Leading Professionals

California, Carolinas, Chicago, Colorado, Florida, Georgia, Great Lakes, London, Minnesota, New England, New York, Pacific Northwest, South Florida, Southwest, Toronto, Western Canada

Art of Celebration Series

Inspiration and Ideas from Top Event Professionals

Chicago & the Greater Midwest, Colorado, Georgia, New England, New York, Northern California, South Florida, Southern California, Southern Style, Southwest, Toronto, Washington, D.C.

City by Design Series

An Architectural Perspective

Atlanta, Charlotte, Chicago, Dallas, Denver, New York, Orlando, Phoenix, San Francisco, Texas

Wineries Series

A Captivating Tour of Established, Estate and Boutique Wineries

California's Central Coast, Napa Valley, New York, Ontario, Sonoma County, Texas, Washington, Napa Valley Iconic Wineries

Experience Series

The Most Interesting Attractions, Hotels, Restaurants, and Shops

Austin & the Hill Country, Boston, British Columbia, Chicago, Southern California, Twin Cities

Interiors Series

Leading Designers Reveal Their Most Brilliant Spaces

Florida, Midwest, New York, Southeast, Washington, D.C., Luxurious Interiors

Golf Series

The Most Scenic and Challenging Golf Holes

Arizona, Colorado, Ontario, Pacific Northwest, Southeast, Texas, Western Canada, Colonial: The Tournament

Weddings Series

Captivating Destinations and Exceptional Resources Introduced by the Finest Event Planners

Southern California

Innovative Interiors Series

Timeless To Trendsetting Commercial Interiors by Leading Architects And Designers

Carolinas, Florida, Midwest, New York, Southern California

Luxury Homes Series

High Style From the Finest Architects and Builders

Carolinas, Chicago, Florida

Specialty Titles

Publications by Architects, Interior Designers, Vintners, Event Planners, Golf Pros and Hoteliers

21st Century Homes, Distinguished Inns of North America, Into the Earth: A Wine Cave Renaissance, Shades of Green Tennessee, Spectacular Hotels, Spectacular Restaurants of Texas, Visions of Design

Custom Titles

Publications by Architects, Interior Designers, Vintners, Event Planners, Golf Pros and Hoteliers

Cloth and Culture: Couture Creations of Ruth E. Funk, Dolls Etcetera, Geoffrey Bradfield Ex Arte, Lake Highland Preparatory School: Celebrating 40 Years, Family Is All That Matters

Panache Books App

Inspiration at Your Fingertips

Download the Panache Books app in the iTunes Store to access select Panache Partners publications. Each book offers inspiration at your fingertips.

Panache Partners, LLC   1424 Gables Court   Plano, Texas 75075   469.246.6060   www.panache.com

INDEX